Ancient Eastern Ph...

FOR BEGINNERS

Richard Osborne and Borin Van Loon

Edited by Richard Appignanesi

ICON ▸ BOOKS

Published in 1996 by Icon Books Ltd.,
52 High Street, Trumpington, Cambridge CB2 2LS

Distributed in the UK, Europe and Asia by the Penguin Group:
Penguin Books Ltd, 27 Wrights Lane, London W8 5TZ

Published in Australia in 1996 by Allen & Unwin Pty. Ltd.,
PO Box 8500, 9 Atchison Street, St. Leonards, NSW 2065

Originating editor: Richard Appignanesi

ISBN 1 874166 34 X

Printed and bound in Great Britain by
The Bath Press, Avon

What is Eastern philosophy? How is it different to Western philosophy? Can Westerners understand Eastern philosophy, given the huge cultural and language difference between the East and the West? These are some of the very tricky questions we will be getting at in this guide to beginning Eastern philosophy.

We said "getting at" rather than answering, because as good philosophers we can never be sure to have completely, or partially, answered the question!

Philosophy, we might say, is the search for knowledge and for a means to express it, and Eastern philosophy has many forms of both.

So, What is Eastern Philosophy?

One answer would be that it is a vast collection of philosophical and religious ideas that derive from the ancient cultures of India, China, Persia, Japan, Korea, Egypt, Tibet, etc, and from many different traditions and forms of thought that shaped the development of the East from earliest recorded times.

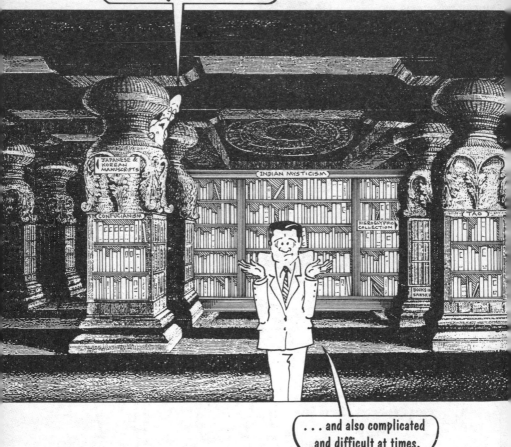

It is also the most ancient tradition of knowledge known to man . . .

. . . and also complicated and difficult at times.

Eastern philosophy is a multi-faceted set of ideas that deeply reflect the complex societies they grew out of.

So, all you need to know is the complex history of the Eastern world, how to speak several languages, read forty thousand volumes of Sanskrit and Chinese, meditate and sit in one position for nine years without moving.

Who knows his own nature knows heaven. So what is our true self? That is the central question.
—Sankara

But you have to start somewhere . . . and in one sense, Eastern philosophy is exactly the same as Western philosophy in that it tries to explain the world we live in and what shapes it. It just comes up with different answers!

Beginning Somewhere . . .

But the question still remains of beginning **somewhere** in Eastern philosophy, of limiting the area to manageable proportions for the beginner. Here is a map that shows some of the origins of Eastern thought and also just how extensive, both in space and time, the subject is.

Where does the "East" begin anyway?

Should we include the Near East and therefore ancient Egypt, dating back to circa 3,000 B.C.?

And what about the other ancient Near Eastern civilizations, Sumer, Babylonia, or indeed the influential ideas of ancient Judaism?

ROMANIA

BLACK SEA

CASPIAN SEA

GREECE

TURKEY

SYRIA

ISRAEL

PERSIA

AFGHANIS

PAKISTAN

EGYPT

LIBYA

RED SEA

SAUDI / ARABIA

How do we class Persian Zoroastrianism which evolved in the 6th century B.C.?

Or later on, the immense impact of Islam and its many schools of thought, including Sufism?

SUDAN

ETHIOPIA

AFRICA

We'll begin somewhere by looking at the oldest and the biggest, **India** and **China**, the birthplaces of the two most ancient, fundamental and systematic traditions of Eastern thought.

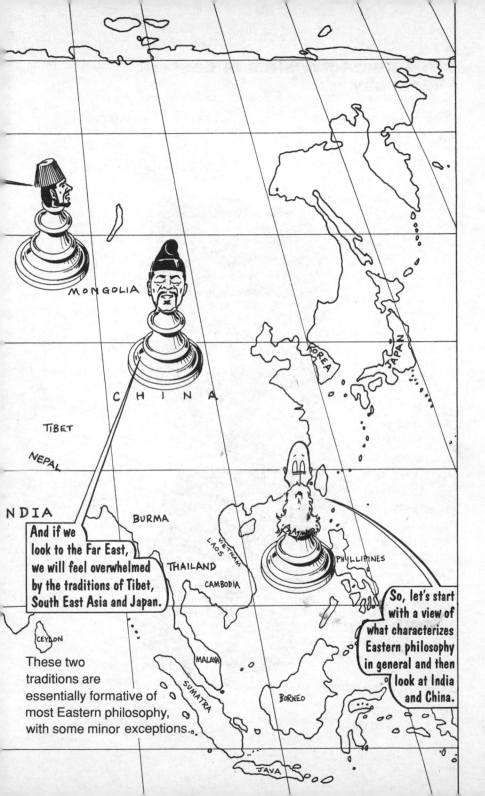

The 4 Characteristics of Eastern Philosophy

To begin with, we can say that Eastern philosophy is characterized by four main aims.

> A cosmological unity, a concern with the timeless realities that lie behind everyday appearances, with self-deliverance and with ethical behaviour.

The big questions are :

What is the true essence of man and how should he transcend the turmoil of earthly life?

What is the true reality?

> To put it another way, the aim of all living is self-definition.

To sum up, the three main strands are Chinese, Indian and Japanese, and there are major differences as well as similarities.

Eastern philosophy has been concerned with suffering, the self, the sublime and the nature of everlasting being.

Man is part of the never-ending cycle of being and death (Hindus call it **Samsara**). No one can escape that reality. But man also lives in society and must contend with that. There are many differences in expressing the way of Enlightenment and the nature of being. Eastern philosophy has a very different notion of the self to Western philosophy, one that accepts the never-ending reality of an all-existing truth.

Is that the idea that liberation comes from getting away from the false self and finding the true self?

That is one of the approaches within Eastern philosophy. There are many paths, but only one road!

East or West . . . Which is Best?

Is it true that Western philosophy grew out of Eastern philosophy?

Which came first is not a question for philosophers, but for historians. There are those who say that in fact all Western philosophy and religion ultimately derived from ancient Eastern wisdom, but we do not know.

Aristotle

Eastern and Western traditions in philosophy have often intersected throughout the ages. In fact, the survival of ancient Greek philosophy owed much to Arab scholars during the Middle Ages.

Unfortunately, we tend to divide the world up into these two great traditions, Eastern and Western, and we all like to think in opposites, good/bad, black/white, right/wrong, etc.

That we are perhaps reaching a stage where these oppositions may be overcome is indicative either of a spiritual re-awakening or a truly global market, or both.

The Eastern world is the "other" that the West has always misunderstood and attempted to dominate.

Now the West needs to understand it because it fears that the East might come to dominate it!

Is Eastern Philosophy just Religion?

Perhaps the one major distinction between Eastern and Western philosophy is that the Eastern tradition does not attempt to distinguish clearly between philosophy and religion. This, of course, leads to some problems. For example, Buddhism as a philosophy is often confused with the religious practices that grew out of it.

We could say that in Eastern thought, true philosophical thinking is essentially religious in its search for truth.

This makes it very different to Western philosophy in which "belief" and "knowledge" have never been on friendly terms.

Eastern Philosophy v. Western Philosophy?

Since the two traditions are always thought of in opposition to each other, it is perhaps worth looking again at some of the similarities and differences.

The search for knowledge in Eastern philosophy has always been more holistic, and less scientific, in the strictly empirical sense, than in Western philosophy.

Against this, we could say that Western philosophy has always been more concerned with truth, logic, reason and independence.

Where Western science has sought absolute Truth in **rationality**, Eastern philosophy has sought complete **Enlightenment** through reflection.

Western philosophy has always tended to over-emphasize the individual and individual things.

Indeed, to ignore the underlying unity of all things is like hitting one locust in a plague.

In Western philosophy, once God was abandoned only reason remained, and science became the new God.

Indeed science and materialism go hand in hand and knowledge of true realities recedes further and further.

Advocates of Eastern philosophy point out exactly where Western science has got us – in a terrible environmental mess in which we need the insights of Eastern philosophy to bring us back into harmony with the earth and the cosmos.

As a general description of the difference between the two great traditions, we can say that the Eastern tends to look inward for the essential answers about man whilst the Western looks outward to the absolute and to the social and political. At the same time, Eastern thought resolutely believes in the interconnectedness of all things and of the need to escape from the limits of individualism, which is connected with bodily pleasures and the illusion of separateness.

What is Real?

Hegel, a great Western philosopher, said . . .

What is rational is actual and what is actual is rational.

Whereas the book of the Tao says . . .

Those who know do not say; those who say do not know.

Hegel probably means that only those things that can be coherently, sensibly argued for can be proven and taken as the real. The Tao probably means that the true nature of ultimate reality is almost unknowable and probably impossible to communicate. (Oddly enough, there are influences of Eastern philosophy in Hegel, but that is another story.)

In contrast to the Western idealization of power, money and science, Eastern traditions have honoured the thinker, the sage, the poet and the mystic. Eastern traditions declare the reality of the unseen world and venerate the call of spiritual life. This is a very fundamental difference.

India: Language Distribution

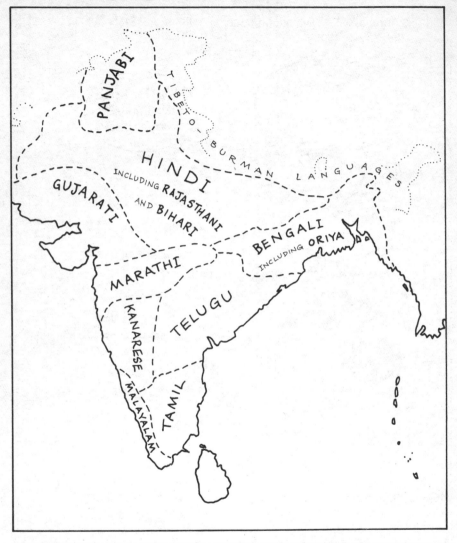

The Indian subcontinent is about half the size of the USA and in more modern times contains about one fifth of the human race. The various religions are represented in the following proportions:*

Hindus	216,000,000
Buddhists	11,000,000
Moslems	68,000,000

India: Race Divisions

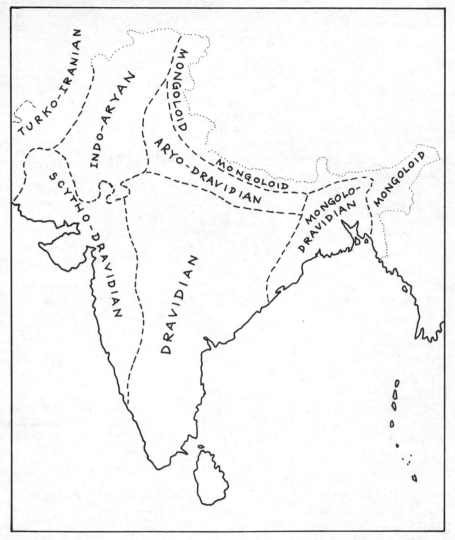

Animists	9,000,000
Christians	4,000,000
Sikhs	3,000,000
Jains	1,000,000
Parsees	101,800
Jews	21,000

1921 census; later censuses show similar proportions.

Indian Philosophy at a Glance

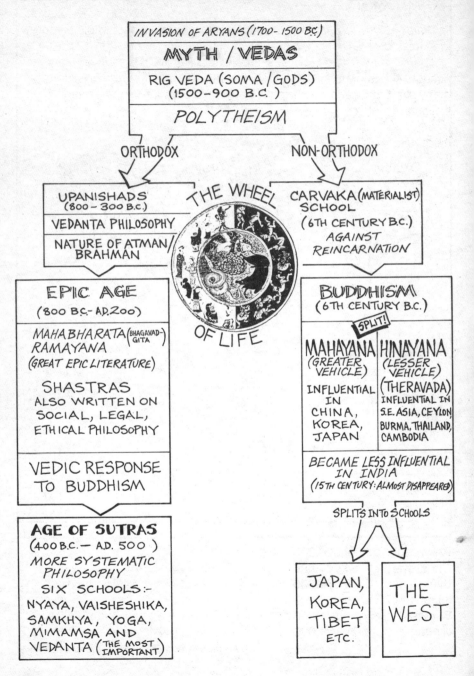

INVASION OF ARYANS (1700-1500 B.C.)

MYTH / VEDAS

RIG VEDA (SOMA / GODS)
(1500–900 B.C.)

POLYTHEISM

ORTHODOX — NON-ORTHODOX

UPANISHADS
(800–300 B.C.)

VEDANTA PHILOSOPHY

NATURE OF ATMAN /
BRAHMAN

THE WHEEL OF LIFE

CARVAKA (MATERIALIST)
SCHOOL
(6TH CENTURY B.C.)
*AGAINST
REINCARNATION*

EPIC AGE
(800 B.C.- A.D. 200)

MAHA BHARATA (BHAGAVAD-GITA)
RAMAYANA
(GREAT EPIC LITERATURE)

SHASTRAS
ALSO WRITTEN ON
SOCIAL, LEGAL,
ETHICAL PHILOSOPHY

VEDIC RESPONSE
TO BUDDHISM

BUDDHISM
(6TH CENTURY B.C.)

SPLIT!

MAHAYANA
(GREATER
VEHICLE)
INFLUENTIAL
IN
CHINA,
KOREA,
JAPAN

HINAYANA
(LESSER
VEHICLE)
(THERAVADA)
INFLUENTIAL IN
S.E. ASIA, CEYLON
BURMA, THAILAND,
CAMBODIA

BECAME LESS INFLUENTIAL
IN INDIA
(15TH CENTURY: ALMOST DISAPPEARED)

SPLITS INTO SCHOOLS

AGE OF SUTRAS
(400 B.C. — A.D. 500)
*MORE SYSTEMATIC
PHILOSOPHY*
SIX SCHOOLS:-
NYAYA, VAISHESHIKA,
SAMKHYA, YOGA,
MIMAMSA AND
VEDANTA (THE MOST
IMPORTANT)

JAPAN,
KOREA,
TIBET
ETC.

THE
WEST

Some Key Characteristics of Indian Philosophy

1) History, myth, religion and philosophy constantly interact within a very long tradition.
2) There are two main schools, **Hindu** and **Buddhist**. The former accepts the authority of the *Vedas*, the latter does not. There are still many similarities and overlaps, however, and both philosophies seek Enlightenment.
3) Almost all Indian philosophies seek Enlightenment through self-discovery (except the materialist schools which reject reincarnation). THE KEY PHRASE IS:

TAT TVAM ASI
= THAT YOU ARE.

Which means discovering your essence or true nature.
4) Within the main traditions, there are many schools of thought with a complex philosophical language that requires much study to understand fully. (We will just look at some of them.)
5) Most Indian philosophy is anti-empirical and concerned with an ultimate reality.
6) Hinduism does not have one founder and one truth but is a complex amalgam of many approaches.
7) Suffering, salvation and the ultimate reality are cornerstones of most Indian philosophizing.
8) In contrast with the absolute monotheism of Western religions, Hinduism is characterized by polytheism and pantheism – many gods, many voices.

Development of the *Vedas*

We need to begin probably some 5,000 years before Christ, when primitive ideas about natural gods began to form a coherent tradition.

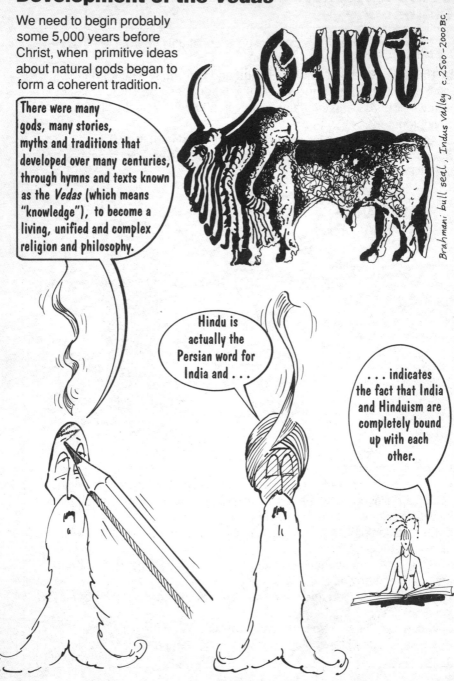

There were many gods, many stories, myths and traditions that developed over many centuries, through hymns and texts known as the *Vedas* (which means "knowledge"), to become a living, unified and complex religion and philosophy.

Brahmani bull seal, Indus Valley c.2500–2000 BC.

Hindu is actually the Persian word for India and . . .

. . . indicates the fact that India and Hinduism are completely bound up with each other.

Despite all the complexities, we should remember one thing . . .

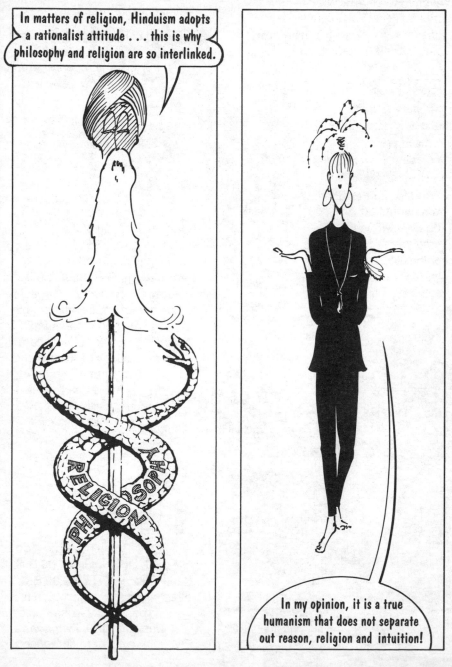

In matters of religion, Hinduism adopts a rationalist attitude . . . this is why philosophy and religion are so interlinked.

In my opinion, it is a true humanism that does not separate out reason, religion and intuition!

Indian philosophical and religious history can be roughly divided into seven main phases.

1) **Prehistoric** and mythic age – era of primitive religions.

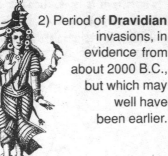

2) Period of **Dravidian** invasions, in evidence from about 2000 B.C., but which may well have been earlier.

3) The **Vedic Period**, from about 1500 to 700 B.C., when the *Vedas* were composed. The *Upanishads* were also written during this era

and are sometimes called the **Vedanta**, or the "end of the *Vedas*", summing up everything in the philosophy of the *Vedas*. Upanishad means something like "sitting down near", which suggests the teacher and pupil relationship as a method of transmitting knowledge. In the *Upanishads*, the notions of **Atman** and **Brahman** are properly elaborated.

SCENES FROM THE RAMAYANA

4) The **Epic Age**, circa 800 B.C. to 200 B.C., in which the beautifully written epics *Mahabharata*, *Ramayana*, etc., were composed.

5) **Age of Sutras**, circa 400 B.C. to A.D. 500. Philosophical thinking became organized through the composition of short **sutras** – or sayings – that could be easily memorized. Different schools developed.

6) **Age of Commentaries**, circa A.D. 400 to A.D.1700, in which the main schools were developed through rigorous commentaries on various sutras. **Sankara** is a major figure here.

7) The era of Renaissance and European influences. Internal influences included the **Bhakti** movements (which were devotional), Islam and Christianity, British imperialism, modernization and science, and of course the rise of Indian nationalism. The British ruled India for hundreds of years but probably never understood it.

Indian Diversity

The main thing about Hinduism and Indian philosophy is that they do not claim one master, one truth and one revealed wisdom, but **many**. This diversity is unusual in world religions and civilizations and is probably due both to the very mixed ethnic groups and invasions of India throughout its history and to its incredibly varied climate, geography and customs.

So Indian philosophy can be defined as coherent, inasmuch as it reflects both the one and the many that is Hinduism, historically and contemporaneously.

Because of the complex traditions of Indian philosophy, much of it can only be understood in relation to the other schools and debates, which is probably why there hasn't already been an *Indian Philosophy for Beginners*!

Indian civilization is one of the seven wonders of the world. It may also be true that the great periods of human history are marked by a widespread access of spiritual energy derived from the fusion of national cultures with foreign influences. To put this another way . . .

India has been at the crossroads of trade, culture and religion for thousands of years, and its ability to absorb, adapt and redefine its own beliefs is the strength of its philosophical tradition.

The Aryan *Vedas*

Hinduism derived from ancient Vedic religions brought to India by people who called themselves **Aryans**. They arrived in India in waves between 2000 and 1000 B.C. The *Vedas* were transmitted in the form of cryptic poetry by word of mouth. There was no written language in India before the 4th century B.C. The ***Rig-Veda***, the oldest of them all, was created between 1500 and 900 B.C., which makes it older than any other text of philosophy or religion.

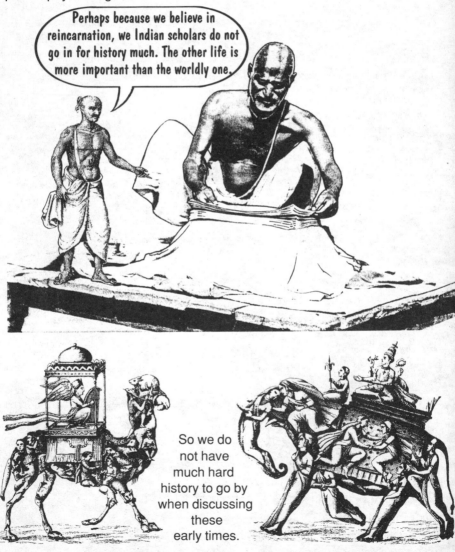

28

Karma and the Caste System

We do know that from the earliest Vedic times there developed a caste system in India which was specific to it.

The caste system is a highly structured set of rules about which social group you belong to, and who you can talk to, marry, work with and so on. Which group you are in depends on your previous lives, how good you'd been and therefore the state of your **karma**. If you are a "lowest of the low", it must be because of the effects of your previous lives.

Basically it was thought up by the Aryans when they invaded India and called all the locals a load of "**Dasas**" (slaves).

A Karmic Hierarchy

At the top of the pile were the **Brahmans** (priests) and at the bottom were the **Sudras**, or servants. In between were the warrior-nobles (**Ksatriyas**) and the merchant farmers (**Vaisyas**). There are many sub-castes and the **Untouchables**, who are completely outside everything.

The notion of karma is a rather difficult philosophical concept we must come back to.

It is not at all clear that the caste system was supported by religion, by the scriptures, by all Brahmans, or by many groups within society. Its rigidity was often broken, sometimes even by the formation of new castes.

Some people argue that it was a combination of racial and economic power that kept the caste system alive . . .

But it is in any case a unique feature of Indian life.

Its longevity and resilience reflect the seeming stability of a civilization that still looks straight back to the poets and philosophers of 3,000 years ago.

Only in this century have real changes begun to emerge.

The truth is that Indian culture is so ancient, so religious and so complex that it defies Western attempts to explain it rationally, which is the only way the West knows how to do it. To be spiritual is not to reject reason but to go beyond it.

GANESH

But why are there so many gods and so many seemingly different approaches to understanding the world?

Because of our history, which is long, complex and interrupted by invasions, we have many religions, many gods and many philosophies. Hinduism combines them all. But there is just one way of realizing that man's true nature is within rather than without, however you express this.

So can I say that Buddhism, Hinduism, different kinds of Yoga, Bhakti, Vishnu, Jaina philosophies and all of these different schools all express a basic philosophical idea?

As the great sages say, Yes and No, or not at all in some respects but in others, and in essence, perhaps.

All Hinduism of whatever variety goes back to the *Vedas*, and there is a Vedanta philosophy which lies at the heart of all Hindu approaches, so you see complexity and simplicity co-exist . . . Put simply, all Hindu and Buddhist thinkers say that **Avidya** (ignorance) is the source of our unhappiness and that **Vidya** (wisdom) and **Bodhi** (Enlightenment) are our salvation. That is a common agreement amongst all Indian thought.

The *Upanishads*

Sometimes called the Vedanta, "end of the *Vedas*", the *Upanishads* are the fullest philosophical expression of the most dominant strand within Hinduism. Mostly belonging to the eighth and seventh centuries B.C., we find in them the monotheism and monism that characterize Hinduism. In these texts, the full philosophical discussion of the nature of Atman and Brahman are first found. The authors of the *Upanishads* and their exact dates are unknown.

WHAT IS KEY IS THE IDEA OF A TRANSCENDENTAL REALITY WHICH IS ALL-INCLUSIVE, BUT NOT A PERSONAL GOD.

In essence we can say that Indian philosophy has, from the very earliest times, been concerned with seeking self-enlightenment through the search for identity.

This search has been a process in which philosophy and religion have always been combined.

Seeking salvation has always meant searching for the higher, or ultimate reality, which lies behind worldly appearances.

BRAHMAN: CREATIVE, PRESERVATIVE & DESTRUCTIVE

More simply, Indian philosophy was not a philosophy of the mind but a philosophy of life in which you had to live the problem of trying to find deliverance.

I've been living the bloody problem for thirty years! I've run 20,000 miles trying to find the answer to the question of why my life is wall-to-wall suffering.
Isn't it because of what you did in a previous life? All that reincarnation stuff?
OK, so the wheel of life means we always live out our previous lives, but I'm always trying to get one step ahead and obey the rules about life's four goals . . .
TO BE VIRTUOUS
TO EXPERIENCE PLEASURE
TO MAKE A LIVING & EVEN BE COMFORTABLE
TO DEVELOP SPIRITUAL AWARENESS

FFICIAL WARNING: Sages say that smoking mess s up your karma
Bastard sahib.

The 4 Stages of Life

Working out how to live occupied Indian philosophers for a very long time – what we call ethics or the problem of what is right or wrong. Orthodox Indians came up very early on with a belief in the four stages of life, described as **student**, **householder**, **forest-dweller** and **hermit**.

Why are there only four? I say there are seven!

These are known as **Asramas** or "rest-stops" which lead to the most important, spiritual awakening, for which one has to become a hermit.

Shakespeare

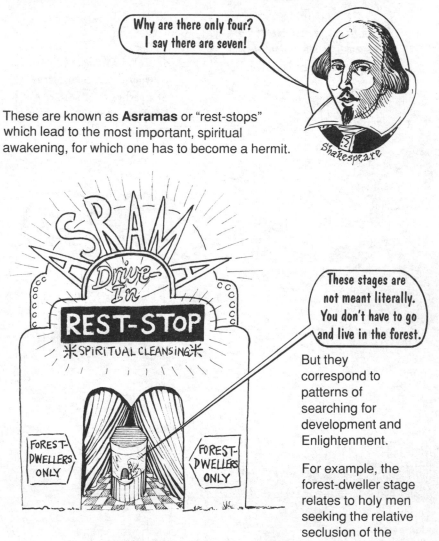

ASRAMA Drive-In

REST-STOP

✳SPIRITUAL CLEANSING✳

FOREST-DWELLERS ONLY

FOREST-DWELLERS ONLY

These stages are not meant literally. You don't have to go and live in the forest.

But they correspond to patterns of searching for development and Enlightenment.

For example, the forest-dweller stage relates to holy men seeking the relative seclusion of the forest to contemplate and meditate.

The Student Stage

This involves a period of intense, disciplined study, mainly of the *Vedas*.

The Householder Stage

The Forest Dweller

This phase involves removing oneself from the pleasures and distractions of everyday life and retreating into a life of contemplation and spiritual awakening.

Again, it is not necessarily a literal "going into the forest".

The Final Stage

Sannyasa, or the hermit stage, is reached when the individual has totally committed himself to spiritual development and cut himself off from the world entirely.

The aim of this phase is to develop **Moksha** or spiritual awareness. To do this, one must be entirely focussed on the higher reality and avoid all contact with everyday life. This kind of Eastern philosophy is sometimes accused of being anti-world and ascetic.

TO FIND THE ABSOLUTE REALITY IS NOT ANTI-WORLDLY BUT A SEARCH FOR TRUTH OR MOKSHA.

44

Karmic Calamity: Women

In case we get too carried away with the brilliance of ancient thought, we should remember that, rather like many Western philosophers, many Veda thinkers saw women as a lower order of being. This was connected to the idea of trying to free oneself from earthly things and desires.

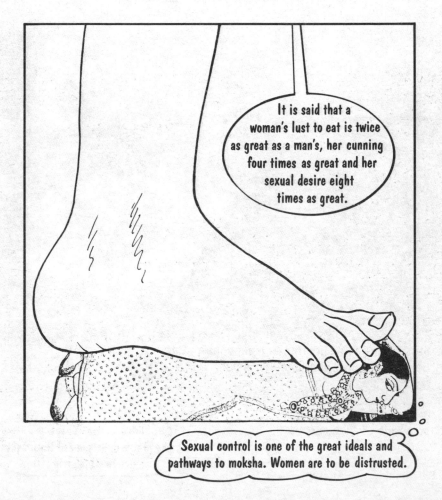

Some of the early Hindu rules about women . . .

1) A female should marry a male three times her age. An ideal age was 8 for the girl and 24 for the man.

2) A girl should marry before her first menstruation, otherwise she was likely to run sexually rampant.

3) Women should not be independent but under the rule first of their fathers, then their husbands, and if their husbands should die, their sons.

4) For women, to fulfil their **Dharma** is to be subservient.

5) Widows should not remarry, but commit **Sati**. Being burnt alive guaranteed blissful reincarnation for wife and husband.

6) A woman must not marry someone of a lower caste.

To be born a woman is seen as a lower place in reincarnation and thus moksha must be a long way off!

One of the more amusing practices that grew out of the idea of avoiding earthly distractions was . . .

To prove one's aloofness one should lie with beautiful naked women in order to show self-control.

Gandhi is said to have done this in the belief that it increased spiritual powers. It probably sharpened the senses, if not leading directly to moksha.

The mind of women brooks no discipline. Her intellect hath little weight...The hearts of women are those of hyenas.
— Indra (Rig Veda)

We're coming next.

Enlightenment clearly seems to have a gender bias.

47

The *Kamasutra*

Although the Upanishadic idea of turning away from the world is a strong one, there is another Hindu saying.

Everyone follows his nature. What can repression accomplish?

The *Kamasutra* is the well-known manual on the sensual art of love-making and accompanies much erotic art in Hindu temples. What are we to make of this seeming contradiction?

Seeking pleasure is legitimate, but it is a baser aim in life. That is why erotic art is on the outside of the temple. You must progress beyond it.

Hinduism does not completely suppress eroticism. It claims to confront and then supersede it by spiritual enlightenment.

We finished so quickly . . .

Some Basic Principles of Vedanta Philosophy

Dharma means law or truth, and also maintenance. The whole Universe is governed by dharma. It covers everything and everybody, from gods to animals, and the ethical conduct of everyone within it. It can also mean the principle of existence. Within the universal framework of moral order, priority is given to the absolute necessity of virtue. Dharma demands that we fulfil our duty in accordance with our specified role – what could be seen as our caste position.

It resembles my universal moral law which dictates how one should behave towards others, not based on a righteous God but on abstract moral principles.

E. Kant

The moral codes derived from dharma can be seen as the ritualization of everyday life.

Dharma must be fulfilled or denied by each individual alone.

49

Moksha basically means genuine spiritual awakening, or the true Enlightenment. It also means liberation from the endless cycle of birth and death (samsara).

This is the aim towards which all the different pathways lead, and what the Buddhists call **Nirvana**. Trying to state clearly that nature of moksha is one of the great philosophical debates within the Indian tradition.

If you can't explain what Enlightenment is, you clearly can't achieve it.

SHIVA NATARAJA, LORD OF THE DANCE

To achieve moksha means to fulfil your duty without being self-interested.

Karma

This is one of the most difficult ideas for Westerners to appreciate, but it is central to all discussions of Indian philosophy.

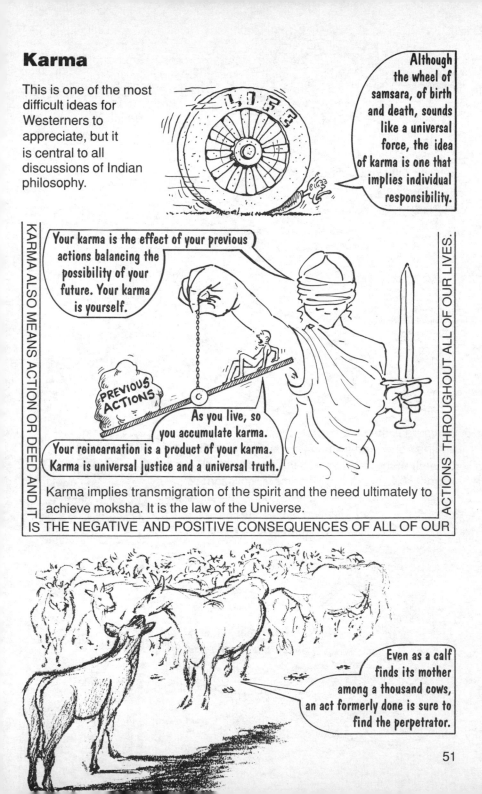

Although the wheel of samsara, of birth and death, sounds like a universal force, the idea of karma is one that implies individual responsibility.

Your karma is the effect of your previous actions balancing the possibility of your future. Your karma is yourself.

PREVIOUS ACTIONS

As you live, so you accumulate karma.
Your reincarnation is a product of your karma.
Karma is universal justice and a universal truth.

Karma implies transmigration of the spirit and the need ultimately to achieve moksha. It is the law of the Universe.

KARMA ALSO MEANS ACTION OR DEED AND IT IS THE NEGATIVE AND POSITIVE CONSEQUENCES OF ALL OF OUR ACTIONS THROUGHOUT ALL OF OUR LIVES.

Even as a calf finds its mother among a thousand cows, an act formerly done is sure to find the perpetrator.

Samsara is the flow of change in all things, or the wheel of life, death and rebirth. Again, an idea which is very alien to Western thinking.

Samsara is the prison in which suffering and pain are the norm, and from which escape must be through many lifetimes and the accumulation of karma. Moksha, or Enlightenment, only comes to the few. Only through the ultimate realization of one's true nature, or Atman, does one escape samsara.

Now a Western perfume, is this some cosmic joke?

EAU DE TOILETTE
un Air de
SAMSARA
GUERLAIN
PARIS

THE SPINNING-WHEEL WAS ORIGINALLY ON THE INDIAN FLAG

The *Bhagavad-gita*

This text is very influential and embodies the ideas of dharma in action. *Bhagavad-gita* literally means "sung by the lord". It is set within the wider framework of the *Mahabharata*, a drama of two warring families, in which many of the philosophical ideas are given concrete realization through the action of the characters. Its 90,000 couplets are often memorized. The central part of the *Bhagavad-gita* concerns **Arjuna** who is about to enter battle but who is racked by doubt about his moral position. His charioteer, **Krishna**, the god in disguise, replies to his uncertainties and in so doing explains much of the notion of dharma.

I am depressed at the coming battle and fearful of the destruction and death that will surely follow.

ARJUNA

KRISHNA

Much of the poem is Krishna's exposition concerning death, reality, duty, action and ultimate understanding.

Elements of the *Bhagavad-gita*

The idea of the **Avatar** – a human intermediary between the gods and mortals. Krishna is both human and divine, a manifestation of the all-pervasive Brahman and of dharma. Thus a moral code, a philosophical idea and a notion of divinity are all expressed within a narrative framework that is comprehensible to all.

I, Arjuna, was blinded by illusion (**Maya**) and ignorance (**Avidya**). I confused my true self with my ego (**Guna**) and must discover my real self (**Atman**).

In counselling Arjuna on behaviour, I, Krishna, stressed that one should not be attached to the results of one's actions. Dharma (duty) must be followed, but in a disinterested way, not for the sake of gaining recognition or glory.

In a very important way, the *Bhagavad-gita* unites and expresses the philosophical ideas of both the *Vedas* and the *Upanishads*. The true revelation is that only in understanding that Brahman is the true underlying principle of reality will all become clear.

The need for action, rather than inaction . . . Recognition of the ultimate reality, of death and re-birth. Since all being is Brahman, and all is Being, there is death — not annihilation but transcendence.

The *Bhagavad-gita* is therefore a model for understanding the philosophical ideas inherent in Vedanta schools. The Vedanta schools all argue the monistic view that all is Brahman.

The Sutra Period and the Six Schools

Called the Sutra period because many of the philosophical ideas that were around at the time were systematized in **sutras** – short sayings that could be easily remembered.

Six Orthodox Hindu Schools		
School	*Founder*	*Text*
Nyaya	Gautama	*Nyaya Sutras* (*c*. 3rd century B.C.–2nd century A.D.)
Vaiseshika	Kanada	*Vaiseshika Sutras* (*c*. 3rd century B.C.–*c*. 100 A.D.)
Samkhya	Kapila (*c*. 7th century B.C.)	*Samkhyapravacana Sutra*
	Isvarakrsna	*Samkhya Karika* (*c*. 3rd century A.D.)
Yoga	Patanjali	*Yoga Sutra* (*c*. 2nd century B.C.)
Mimanisa	Jamuni	*Purva-Mimanisa Sutra* (*c*. 400 B.C.)
Vedanta	Badarayana	*Brahma Sutra* (4th-2nd century B.C.)

The expression "**Darshana**" is used, which means "point of view" and signifies a sense of different philosophical approaches. However, the interpretation of these short sayings was not always clear, and thus the seeds of disputation and argument were laid.

The sutras became the basis of the later commentaries – all debate has to start with them. Wide differences existed between the philosophical schools . . .

The Nyaya and Vaiseshika Schools

Although still covering the same basic ground as other Indian philosophies, the **Nyaya** school advocated proper logical rules for reasoning. (Nyaya means something like "determining the right meaning".) In fact, they were very concerned with knowledge in general. Rather than just asserting things, the Nyaya school developed ways of arguing that are very similar to Western logic. From this kind of philosophy, arguments arose about the East's influence on the West.

My work on logic is very similar to some of the Nyaya school, but we have no idea who might have influenced whom.

Eastern logic certainly came first!

Nyaya states that there are four valid sources of knowledge. Perception, inference, analogy and credible testimony.

Reasoning by SYLLOGISM was important both to the Nyaya and to Aristotle. The form of methodical reasoning adopted by the Nyaya was called the **Tarka**, and operated in five stages.

1) Primary hypothesis.

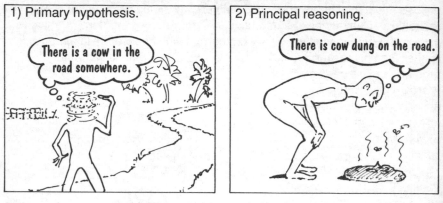

There is a cow in the road somewhere.

2) Principal reasoning.

There is cow dung on the road.

3) Major theory (must have concrete examples).

Where there is dung . . .

. . . there is an animal.

(The premise also includes the relationship between classes of things, animals/dung.)

4) Application. The premise and supporting examples are applied to the particular case.

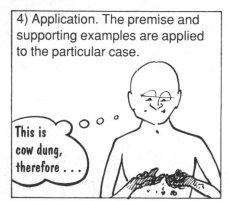

This is cow dung, therefore . . .

5) The conclusion is asserted.

There is no dung without a cow behind it! Therefore there is a cow in the road.

This formal method of reasoning also involves causality (cause and effect), which the Nyaya school were very keen on. The school was later divided into the Old and New Nyaya in the 12th century A.D. as more advances were made.

The Navya Nyaya (New Logic School)

Gangesa founded this influential branch of Eastern learning and logic in the 12th century A.D. Its main thrust was a philosophical analysis that was concerned with logical analysis.

Following on from the sense that what is real can be defined, they were very concerned with how one might define absence, or negation. Quite tricky, that one!

The Vaiseshika School

This school, which overlaps with the Nyaya, argued that physical reality is composed of invisible, indestructible atoms, of which there were four kinds. Again, there is a strange correspondence to ideas that the materialist Greek thinkers later put forward. The idea of this unseen structure of the Universe is used to support the idea that . . .

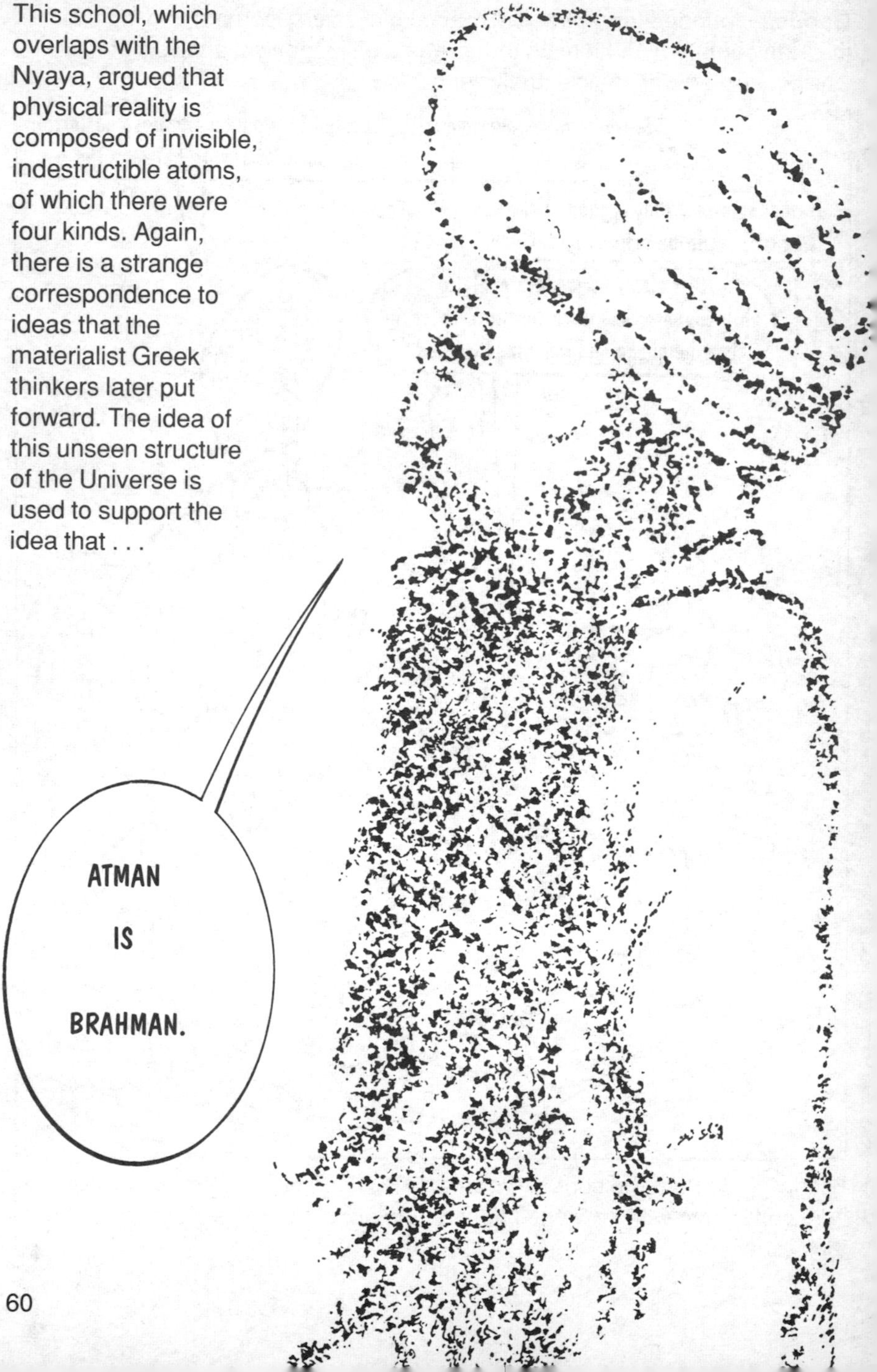

ATMAN

IS

BRAHMAN.

This combination of physics and metaphysics is an interesting one that reappears in modern Indian philosophy. Not everyone liked the school's line of reasoning about physical reality.

Samkhya School

Founded by **Kapila** who, it is thought, lived in the 7th century B.C. One of the most important schools in Eastern philosophy which advocates an interesting and quite complicated dualistic vision of the Universe.

Purusha and Prakriti

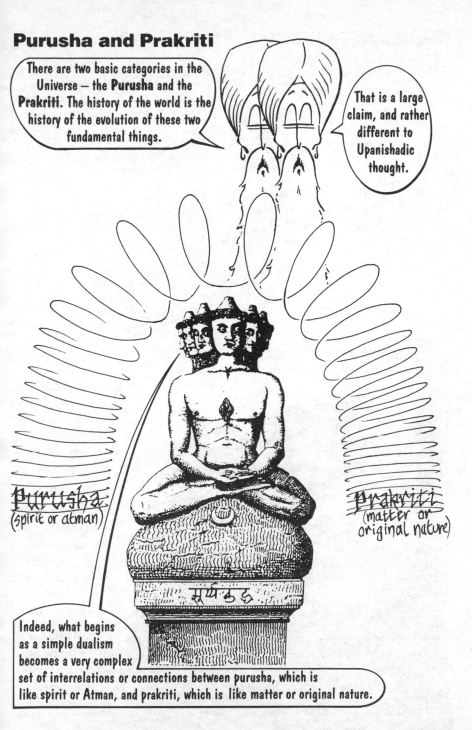

There are two basic categories in the Universe — the **Purusha** and the **Prakriti**. The history of the world is the history of the evolution of these two fundamental things.

That is a large claim, and rather different to Upanishadic thought.

Purusha
(spirit or atman)

Prakriti
(matter or original nature)

Indeed, what begins as a simple dualism becomes a very complex set of interrelations or connections between purusha, which is like spirit or Atman, and prakriti, which is like matter or original nature.

First, one must grasp the nature of purusha. It is spirit, it is many spirits, it is being and consciousness, it is limitless, it is untainted awareness.

ACTIVITY (RAJAS)

INACTIVITY (TAMAS)

TRANSPARENCY (SATTVA)

It is argued that the world is formed as purusha infuses prakriti, and that this stimulates the three states of prakriti. These three states, or **Gunas**, are known as . . .

These forces interact and play different parts in the development of prakriti. As prakriti is activated it becomes **Buddhi** (intellect), out of which individual egos evolve. Individuals often confuse their ego with their true self.

EGO

Liberation can only happen when the true distinction is understood.

True liberation is obtained at death when the bond between the purusha and the prakriti is dissolved.

The Samkhya school also believe strongly in causation, do they not? How does this fit in?

You mean that they argue for cause and effect and for the indestructibility of matter?

Exactly. It is known as the theory of the existent effect, which means that they imply that in the cause of all things the effect already exists.

Doesn't this mean that in some mysterious way the cause of something pre-exists its effect, even though they are distinct things?

Look, take a jar of clay. The jar is the clay but then it is not the lump of clay, clear?

Yoga School

This school is similar to the Samkhya school philosophically, except that a personal God is seen as the mover and shaker of the Universe. In **Yoga**, the search for the true self is both mental and physical. Philosophy and action are combined into a practice which seeks harmony.

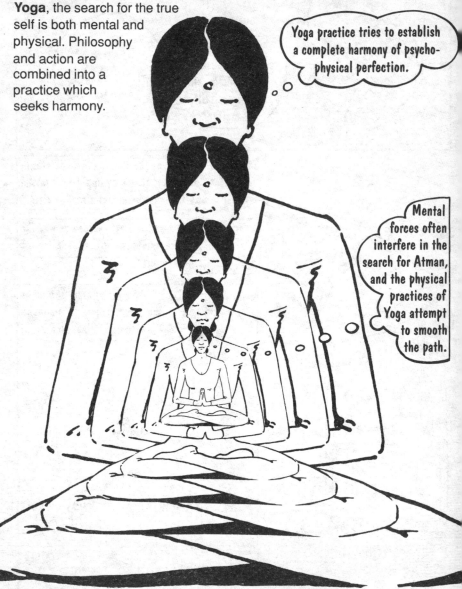

Yoga practice tries to establish a complete harmony of psycho-physical perfection.

Mental forces often interfere in the search for Atman, and the physical practices of Yoga attempt to smooth the path.

One attempts to reach a state of "untainted" knowledge (or Enlightenment) by abandoning the pull of the mind and the body.

The Yogic tradition of disciplined meditation is a matter-of-fact, practical system for achieving Enlightenment. Rather than Enlightenment through knowledge, Yoga seeks to escape from prakriti into pure being (or purusha). The aim is to seek true reality. There are eight ascending steps in the discipline which lead to the **Samadhi** (highest state).

This is a very structured approach, which has also caught on in the West (probably because it is a brilliant way of relieving stress).

And you can learn to fly if you try hard enough!

SAMADHI

MEDITATION

PROPER CONCENTRATION

SUBSIDING OF SENSES

PROPER BREATHING

PROPER POSTURE

GOOD BEHAVIOUR

SELF-DISCIPLINE (A GOOD START)

Advaita-Vedanta School

Vedanta means the "end of the *Vedas*" and **Advaita** means philosophical **monism**, or the idea that reality is one thing, not divisible. In the person of **Sankara** this notion was fully developed around the end of the 8th century A.D. This is certainly the most influential school in Hindu philosophy.

> All that exists is God, and all that exists of us is really God, that is, that part of us that really exists is God, and is called Atman.

The Advaita school can be said to be based on three main texts:

Badarayana's

Brahma Sutra — The Upanishads — Bhagavad-Gita

Understanding the nature of Brahman is obviously the key philosophical problem, and not one that is easily achieved.

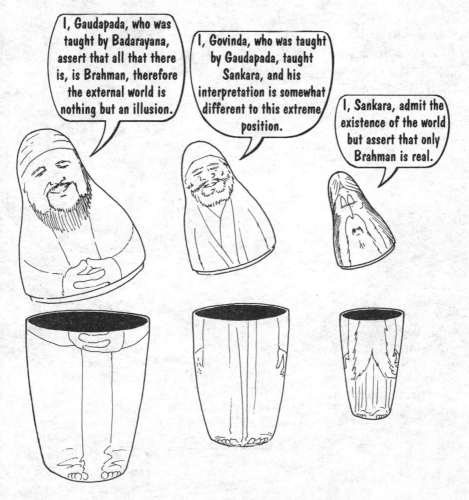

I, Gaudapada, who was taught by Badarayana, assert that all that there is, is Brahman, therefore the external world is nothing but an illusion.

I, Govinda, who was taught by Gaudapada, taught Sankara, and his interpretation is somewhat different to this extreme position.

I, Sankara, admit the existence of the world but assert that only Brahman is real.

70

The relationship between the world and Brahman is clearly quite a tricky one and in fact sometimes the argument is that it is inexpressible, or **Maya**. It brings us back to the question of:

The answer is that without Brahman there can be no world, but of course Brahman does not depend on the nature of the appearance of the world. So, to make statements about Brahman means they must have an empirical form, but in one sense these are an illusion, like the snake was. Brahman can be viewed in two ways: as **Nirguna**, without characteristics, and as **Saguna**, with characteristics.

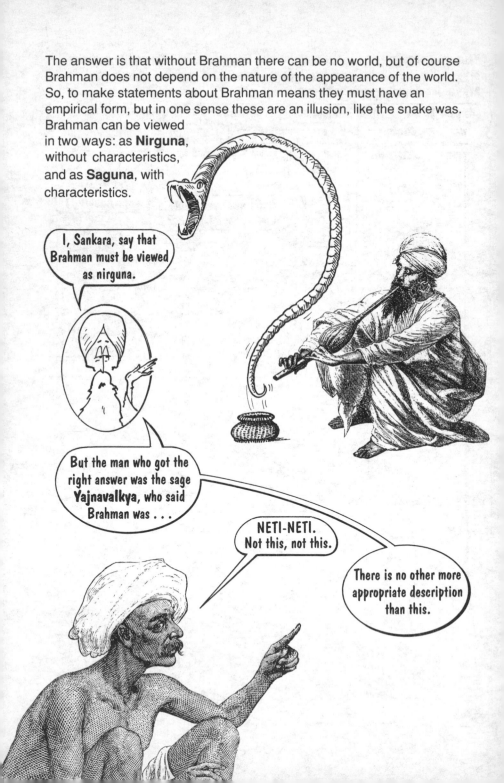

I, Sankara, say that Brahman must be viewed as nirguna.

But the man who got the right answer was the sage **Yajnavalkya**, who said Brahman was . . .

NETI-NETI. Not this, not this.

There is no other more appropriate description than this.

Sankara argued that Brahman and Atman are one, and that Brahman is the cause of the world, but that somehow the world is only a manifestation of its original cause.

The point is that Brahman is the cause of the world in an entirely dispassionate way, without concern for the consequences. Only, Brahman remains real.

Which brings us back to saying, "Tat tvam asi". Our reality is guaranteed by discovering our true self, which is Atman. Atman is Brahman.

Medieval and Later Indian Thought

Indian thought continued to develop, but always with reference back to the original texts and positions. **Ramanuja** (1056–1137) and **Madhva** (1197–1276) were two scholars who later put forward reinterpretations of the *Upanishads*. Ramanuja believed in what is called a **qualified nondualism**.

> I, Ramanuja, believe that reality can be seen as composed of three fundamental entities . . .

ISHVARA OR GOD

WORLD OR MATTER

JIVA OR INDIVIDUAL SOULS

The world and souls are manifestations of God, or Ishvara (Brahman), but they are distinct from it. So he is arguing that God is everything, but that the body and the soul are attributes of God, they qualify God, but are distinct. His main point is that Brahman can only be known through its attributes, or in other words through the world.

> So the world and God exist, but only God is pure substance.

> I was a bit worried there for a moment. I thought I was going to unexist again.

Madhva (13th Century)

Madhva argued for the dualism of Brahman and Jiva (individual souls). He opposed Sankara's nondualism and said that all things are different.

There are five fundamental distinctions in reality . . .

VISHNU & LAKSHMI ON THE BIRD GUD GARUDA

VISHNU THE CREATOR

1) God and matter.

2) God and the soul.

3) The soul and matter.

4) Between different souls.

5) Between different forms of matter.

Madhva views God as **Vishnu** and as completely transcendent, as the only self-sufficient reality on which everything else is reliant. His philosophical ideas were later utilized by the Bhakti devotional movements which approached God not through knowledge, but through simple devotion.

75

Jainism

This school was traditionally founded by **Vardhamana Mahavira** (599–527 B.C.). Its approach elevated an absolute respect for life, as well as the idea of non-violence or **Ahimsa**.

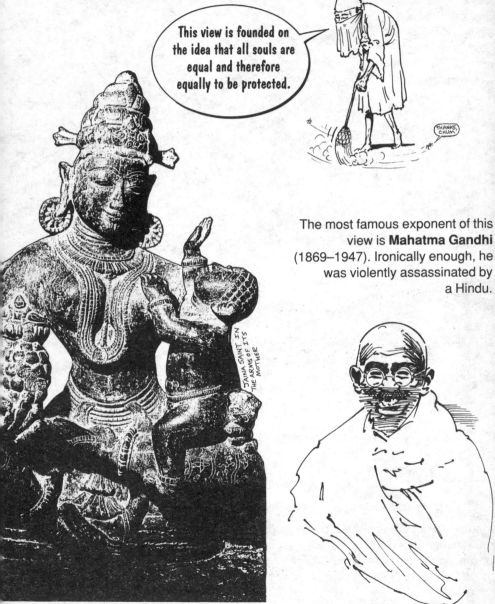

This view is founded on the idea that all souls are equal and therefore equally to be protected.

THANKS, CHUM.

JAINA SAINT IN THE ARMS OF ITS MOTHER

The most famous exponent of this view is **Mahatma Gandhi** (1869–1947). Ironically enough, he was violently assassinated by a Hindu.

The **Jaina** code of conduct was aimed, like Buddhism, at escaping from the endless wheel of life (samsara), and involved the Three Jewels:

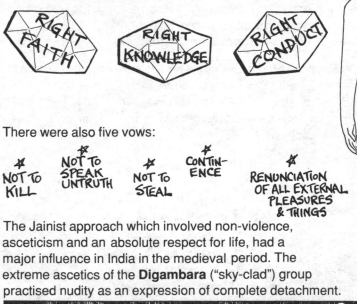

There were also five vows:

NOT TO KILL · NOT TO SPEAK UNTRUTH · NOT TO STEAL · CONTINENCE · RENUNCIATION OF ALL EXTERNAL PLEASURES & THINGS

JAIN AUSTERITY

The Jainist approach which involved non-violence, asceticism and an absolute respect for life, had a major influence in India in the medieval period. The extreme ascetics of the **Digambara** ("sky-clad") group practised nudity as an expression of complete detachment.

This never caught on in the northern provinces.

Buddhism

Although Buddhism is opposed to the philosophy of the *Vedas*, and to what it sees as its metaphysical abstractness, it is based in Hindu traditions. It is less strictly philosophical than many of the schools, being more concerned with practical liberation from suffering. (See the excellent ***Buddha for Beginners***.)

Buddhist teachings are based on what are called the Three Jewels of Buddhism: the **Buddha**, the **Dharma**, and the **Sangha**. The life of Buddha himself is the first jewel, and the story of his searching for truth forms the prime example of his teachings.

Naturally it is very difficult to distinguish myth and reality when discussing my life, much like Jesus or any other number of saints and holy men.

The Buddha

Buddha (otherwise known as **Siddhartha Gautama**) lived 536–476 B.C. and finally obtained Enlightenment sitting under a tree in the town of Bodh Gaya. His "awakening" led to the second jewel, the Dharma.

I called for a different route to Enlightenment. One which concerned itself with the nature of suffering in the world.

Buddha wandered about for forty-nine years after his "awakening", spreading the gospel and the idea of achieving "nirvana".

Could one say that Buddhism was the practical application of the Hindu ideas of asceticism and escaping from samsara?

You could, but it would only be half right. Buddhism is clearly derived from the *Vedas*, but then it rejects several of the key ideas of Vedantic philosophy.

The third jewel, the Sangha, is the Buddhist Order itself, the Community of Monks. It is the means by which the faith is organized, and so we are not too concerned with it.

The third jewel, the Sangha, is the Buddhist Order itself, the Community of Monks. It is the means by which the faith is organized, and so we are not too concerned with it.

79

The Four Noble Truths

The Dharma is expressed by the **Four Noble Truths**, and the part known as the **Middle Way**, which sounds rather like what Aristotle called the Golden Mean. The Four Noble Truths are . . .

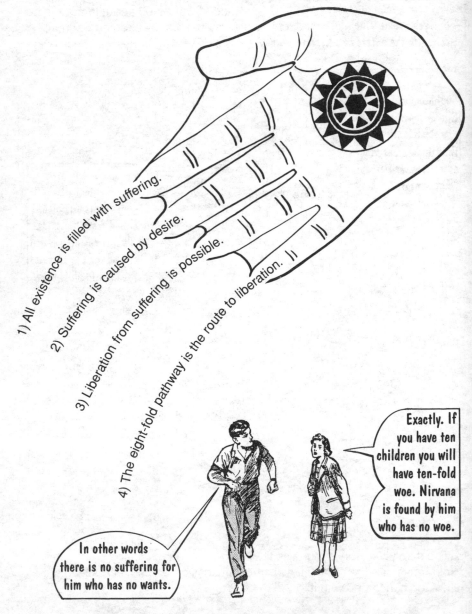

1) All existence is filled with suffering.

2) Suffering is caused by desire.

3) Liberation from suffering is possible.

4) The eight-fold pathway is the route to liberation.

In other words there is no suffering for him who has no wants.

Exactly. If you have ten children you will have ten-fold woe. Nirvana is found by him who has no woe.

Buddhism avoided the ritual and élitism of Vedic approaches, teaching in the common languages of the day and supporting an egalitarian approach to Enlightenment.

This probably explains some of Buddhism's success around the world.

Yet Buddhism didn't fare all that well in India itself, but became a very important force in many parts of Asia and the East, particularly China and Japan, which we'll come to later.

Differences between Buddhism and Vedic Thought

The Self in Buddhism

The orthodox schools of Hindu philosophy are all concerned with the nature of the self, and with the notion that Atman is Brahman. Buddhism takes a completely different line.

Buddhism asserts that there is no unique individual self. This philosophical position is very radical and, of course, difficult for Westerners to take on board.

The Buddhist Idea of Rebirth

Buddhists, in other words, argue that there is **Anatman**, or no-self. This radical empiricism may well be part of the reason that Buddhism fell out of favour in India.

If there is no-self, why do Buddhists believe in rebirth? How can something that does not exist be reborn?

What Buddhists argue is that through what they call **dependent origination**, in which everything is the cause and effect of everything else, including the self, an illusion of the continuity of the self is created.

There is rebirth, as there is karma, but it is not the rebirth of an independent soul.

The Buddhist philosophical position is based on the idea that there is a continuity, there are links from one existence to another, but that the "self" is an illusion created by the combination of mental and physical activities. Meditation is a way of approaching the mind as pure mind, to get past the illusion of self.

Consciousness is the combination of the many forms and states of being which are like a stream of impressions, Ideas and sensations. Mind links these states that are thought of as the "person", but only mind exists through rebirth.

Karma links the lives of man and is the most important part in the self.

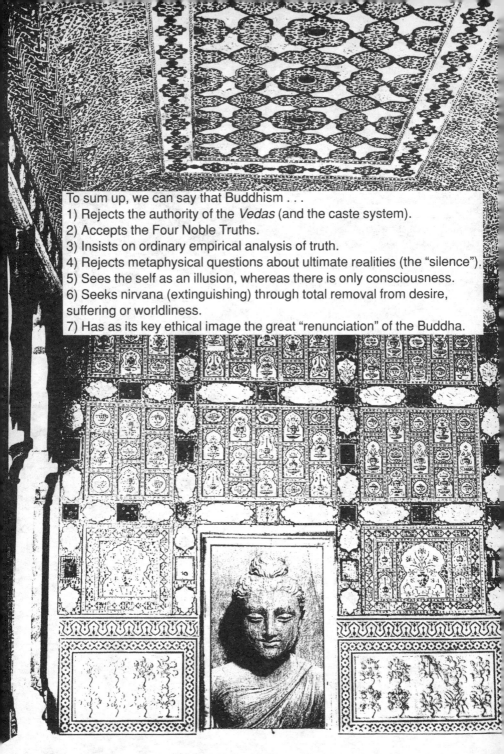

To sum up, we can say that Buddhism . . .
1) Rejects the authority of the *Vedas* (and the caste system).
2) Accepts the Four Noble Truths.
3) Insists on ordinary empirical analysis of truth.
4) Rejects metaphysical questions about ultimate realities (the "silence").
5) Sees the self as an illusion, whereas there is only consciousness.
6) Seeks nirvana (extinguishing) through total removal from desire, suffering or worldliness.
7) Has as its key ethical image the great "renunciation" of the Buddha.

The Spread of Buddhism from India

Buddhism had a great influence all over the Eastern world, and, in more modern times, in Western countries.

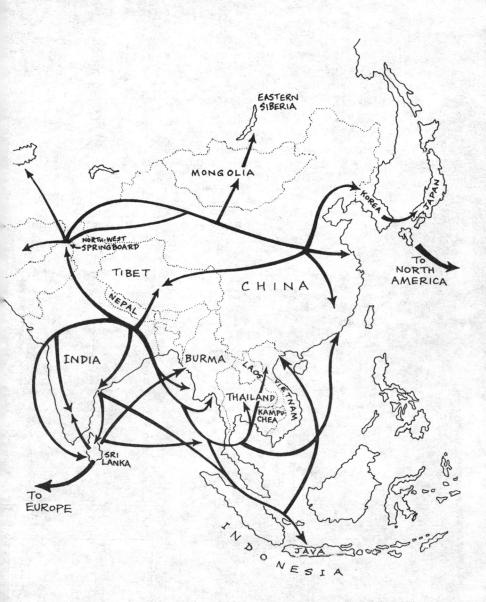

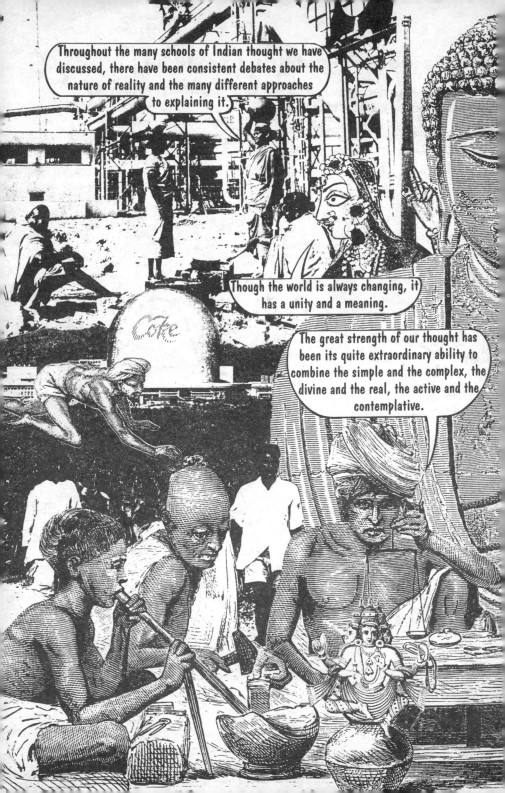

China and Philosophy

To consider China and its philosophy is to make another giant leap, because Chinese culture, although Eastern, is markedly different to Indian. What fundamentally distinguishes Chinese culture is its sense of harmony, interconnectedness, language and continuity. China has a cult of the Old in which tradition is everything.

Except when they have revolutions!

Confucianism is a very different cultural force to Hinduism.

Heaven and earth, man and family, reason and intuition, Yin and Yang, these things are not in opposition but strive for harmony.

Chinese Language

In discussing Chinese philosophy we first need to recognize that there is a real problem of translation. The Chinese language is nothing like the Western languages we are used to. Rather than an alphabet it uses characters (or ideographs) which are much less precise than a phonetic and grammatically organized language like Latin.

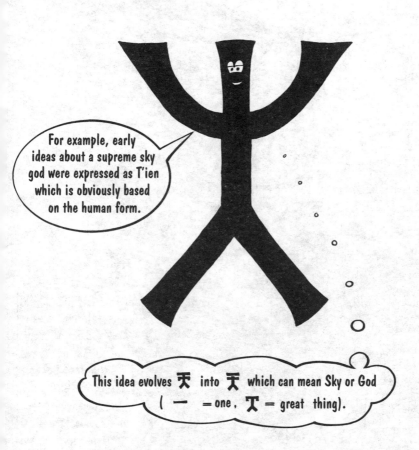

For example, early ideas about a supreme sky god were expressed as T'ien which is obviously based on the human form.

This idea evolves 天 into 天 which can mean Sky or God (一 = one, 大 = great thing).

Chinese is a language much more allusive and dependent on context than Romance languages. It is not a language easily amenable to logical philosophy.

China's Culture

Chinese culture is one of the most ancient and self-contained we know of, and its longevity is one of the key features that mark it out as unique. Its philosophy, rather like Indian philosophies, shows a complexity and unity which incorporates many diverse veins and philosophical strategies that stretch over thousands of years. Unlike India, however, the gods do not loom large in early Chinese civilization.

There are mythologies of early gods, Emperors and Kings, but the gods as such are not of paramount importance.

In philosophical terms, there is a period known as the time of the **Hundred Schools** (400–200 B.C.) in which many different philosophical positions were advanced, but they almost all relied on tradition and past ideas for authority.

The oldest examples go back 3,000 years B.C. We have no idea whether they are entirely true, false or a mixture.

The Role of Philosophy

In Chinese culture, philosophy has played the role that religion plays in the West. What do we mean by this?

Simply that Chinese civilization has always assumed that everyone who has an education will naturally study and understand their traditional philosophies.

There is no state religion, or state church, and religion is not one of the ways in which the Chinese nation defines itself.

Compare this with Italy, the Catholic Church and the Pope.

Chinese culture does not depend on the idea of a God to whom everyone is answerable, nor do its original myths talk about a supernatural creation. Chinese culture is secular and philosophical in the broadest sense.

From the earliest days of Chinese civilization, traditional ways of thinking were passed from generation to generation.

The officials of the Imperial Court had an important role in this.

Traditional ideas were treated with the kind of respect that is often accorded to religion.

It is important to note too that the language of ancient China remained unchanged throughout the centuries, so that Confucius can be understood today in much the same way as 2,500 years ago.

His social ethics have been an important part of official Chinese culture for that whole time.

The language of a culture embodies its deepest roots.

From the earliest times, Confucius had an idea of the man of virtue, the Gentleman (Chun-Tzu), and this defined an ethic, a mode of behaviour and a social order.

Chinese Civilization at a Glance

1) It is the oldest continuous culture in the world (5,000 years old?) and fundamentally an agricultural society.

2) It is a secular and multi-religious civilization.

3) Its language is an important unifying factor, and expresses a particular way of thinking.

4) Confucian philosophy, or ethics, underpins most of later Chinese civilization and culture.

5) Religion and philosophy are closely interwoven and therefore difficult to separate out.

6) Much Chinese philosophy extolled the virtues of wise rulers and a well-governed people.

7) The family, and familial relations, are the basis of Chinese society. (With women at the bottom of the pile.)

The Spirit of Chinese Philosophy

What then is the distinctive spirit of Chinese philosophy? A certain Dr. Fung, who wrote a very long *Short History of Chinese Philosophy*, said that one of the recurring themes was a notion of "Sageliness within and Kingliness without".

To put it in the most general way, Chinese philosophy is down-to-earth. It is not concerned with God, or with absolute truth, but with the question of how to live properly on earth, with ethics, the principles of social living and government.

Chinese philosophy is concerned with the question of man and his ancestors.

Except for Buddhism, which is the opposite!

There are as many kinds of Chinese philosophy as there are clouds in the sky, but heaven enfolds them all.

Main Strands of Chinese Thought

The three over-arching philosophies are **Confucianism**, **Taoism** and **Buddhism**, but they all interact with one another. (A unity in diversity.)

Chinese philosophy is not about accumulating facts, but about elevating human nature, which is a far more difficult task.

An old Chinese saying is: "In office a Confucian, in retirement a Taoist".

Chinese philosophers have always expressed themselves in a peculiar aphoristic manner, not in long-winded argumentation.

BUDDHA

CONFUCIUS

LAOTZU

This is because suggestiveness is one of the great principles of all Chinese art and thinking.

Take this expression:

"A man will stand on a mountain for a thousand years before a duck flies in".

97

The Ancient Dynasties

There are many preconceptions in the West about China, many of them based on the strange reportings of Marco Polo and other Westerners who have imagined China in their travels. Even today we know little about Chinese history. The earliest period we have definite evidence for is the **Shang** dynasty (1766–1123 B.C.). When we reach the **Chou** dynasty (1122–256 B.C.), we reach the period of the greatest historical knowledge and also the Golden Age of Chinese philosophy.

From the creation of the **Ch'in** dynasty in 221 B.C. (from which the name of China comes) until the creation of the Chinese republic in 1912, there was a virtually continuous form of government and culture.

And I was the grandfather, midwife, and original synthesizer of early Chinese ethics and thought.

The Four Phases

We can roughly divide Chinese philosophical history into four major phases.

Ancient Period (before 200 B.C.): Characterized by many competing (The Hundred) schools.
Middle Period (200 B.C.–A.D. 960): Confucianism, Taoism and the introduction of Buddhism.
Neo-Confucianism (960–1912): Reaction to Buddhism, renaissance of Confucianism.
Modern Period (1912–present): Arrival of Western thought, revival of Confucianism and Marxism.

Throughout it all, there is the deep sense of the self-contained continuity of China, or as Confucius put it . . .

The wise man delights in water, the good man delights in mountains. The wise move, the good stay still. The wise are happy, the good endure.

99

Two Main Trends

The values of Chinese society grew out of the "value of agriculture", the family and the state that were based on these two things. There were two main trends, Taoism and Confucianism, which seem the opposite of each other but which constantly interact to produce the dynamic stability of Chinese thought.

This can be expressed as: REVERSAL IS THE MOVEMENT OF TAO.

CONFUCIANISM

TAOISM

This idea flows through Chinese thought like a tidal flood.

It means that anything taken to its extreme, produces a reversal to the other extreme.

The **Book of Changes** (**I Ching**) says:

This sense of development and negation is important in both Confucianism and Taoism.

When the cold goes, the warmth comes, and when the warmth comes, the cold goes.

100

Chinese Humanism

Chinese philosophy was humanistic, by which we mean that it thought of man as being the centre of the Universe. In this sense, Chinese philosophy was very much this-worldly rather than other-worldly. However, if this were wholly true, it would be very difficult to explain why Buddhism became so popular in China. Buddhism is very concerned with leaving this world behind in achieving nirvana.

So, Chinese tradition is both idealistic and realistic. It looks to man by looking at heaven.

Or as one philosopher put it when talking about neo-Confucianism . . .

It is not divorced from daily ordinary activities, yet it goes straight to what antedated Heaven.

The First Scholars

One of the first attempts to describe the Hundred Schools of Chinese philosophy was the *Historical Records* (*Shih Chi*) of **Ssu-ma Ch'ien** who died in 110 B.C. In this great work, he outlined the essential ideas of the previous centuries.

I classed them into six major schools.

A bit later, the scholar **Liu Hsin** (46 B.C.–A.D. 23) prepared a summary of the books in the Imperial Library, and in so doing classified the Hundred Schools into ten main groups (six the same as Ssu-ma Ch'ien).

But I also tried to analyse the history of the different schools.

Already at this point, there were discussions that led back to Yao and Shun, sages supposed to have lived in the 23rd and 24th centuries B.C.

The allusiveness of much Chinese philosophy means that strictly defining the schools of thought is like describing the varieties of grass in a meadow.

Interestingly, Liu Hsin sees the origins of the different schools in the functions of the officers of the Court, or in specific groups and their functions in society. It is almost a "sociological" approach.

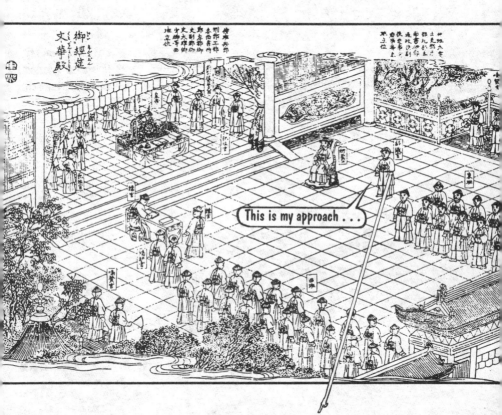

The **Ju** (Confucian school) had their origin in the literati.
The **Yin-Yang** school developed from the cosmologists.
The **Mohist** school had its origins in the knights.
Members of the **Taoist** school came from the hermits.
The **School of Names** came from the professional debaters.
The **Legalist** school came from the "men of methods" (politicians).

Ssu-ma Ch'ien's Divisions

The **Yin-Yang Chia** (Yin-Yang school). Deriving from ancient cosmology, it was concerned with the two basic principles which govern the Universe, now quite well known in the West.

Yin represents the passive female principle and **Yang** the active male. The two constantly interact to create all things and all development.

Yang originally meant sunshine and Yin the opposite, and from this developed a cosmic dualistic approach.

These ideas were later connected with the famous *I Ching* (*Book of Changes*) which described the cosmological principles of the Universe and elaborated them in ways that could be divined through patterns of hexagrams.

This basic idea has many consequences and runs throughout Chinese philosophy.

The Yin-Yang school and its ideas of the natural interplay of universal forces had very deep roots in Chinese popular culture.

The fatalism of much peasant culture is reinforced by the superstitious divination that the *I Ching* elaborates.

However, the Yin-Yang approach led to a scientific view of the natural forces at work in the Universe, as well as the occult view based in divination.

Confucius

The second school is known as the **Ju Chia** (school of the literati), also known as the Confucian school, of whom **Confucius** (551–479 B.C.) was obviously the most important figure.

This school, certainly the most influential, was interested in **human-heartedness** and **righteousness**. Two thousand years before the Renaissance in Europe they put man at the very centre of their thought. Their central question was how could man improve himself and aspire to greatness on this earth. To be a gentleman of learning and distinction was the base line. As Confucius put it in the *Analects* . . .

He cultivates himself so as to bring tranquillity to all the people.

The philosopher sage **K'ung Fu-Tzu** lived about 2,500 years ago and has probably had more influence than any other philosopher in world history. "Confucius" is the Latinized name given to him later. We know little of his real life and are not certain that he actually wrote his famous *Analects* (sayings). The first biography of Confucius was not written until some three hundred years after his death, so its accuracy must be questioned. Certainly, there is a body of knowledge and teachings that are ascribed to Confucius. **Mencius**, who lived a hundred years after the sage and who founded the tradition that bears his name, said of him . . .

Ever since man came into the world there has never been anyone greater than Confucius.

It is said that Confucius worked in Government, and later in his life taught privately. It seems probable that he was one of the first in Chinese history to teach large numbers of students privately (probably thousands), and many of them went on to become famous scholars and thinkers.

The *Six Classics*

The *Six Classics* correspond to the liberal arts (or **Liu Yi**).

The *Book of Changes* (Yi)

MUSIC (Yeuh)

BOOK of HISTORY (Shu)

BOOK OF ODES (Shih)

RITUALS OR RITES (Zhi Li, I Li, Li Ji)

SPRING & AUTUMN ANNALS

But Confucius did write the *Analects*, or least most of them, or perhaps some of them, we think.

The point is not so much what he actually said, but the ways his ideas have been expressed and used during the centuries.

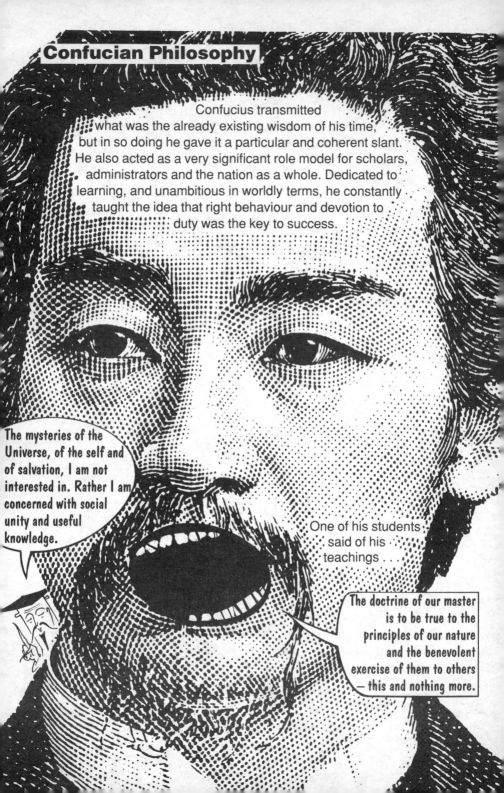

Confucian Philosophy

Confucius transmitted what was the already existing wisdom of his time, but in so doing he gave it a particular and coherent slant. He also acted as a very significant role model for scholars, administrators and the nation as a whole. Dedicated to learning, and unambitious in worldly terms, he constantly taught the idea that right behaviour and devotion to duty was the key to success.

The mysteries of the Universe, of the self and of salvation, I am not interested in. Rather I am concerned with social unity and useful knowledge.

One of his students said of his teachings . . .

The doctrine of our master is to be true to the principles of our nature and the benevolent exercise of them to others — this and nothing more.

Of learning, Confucius said . . .

If by keeping the old warm, one can provide understanding of the new, one is fit to be a teacher.

He also said . . .

If there is education there are no class-distinctions.

He took four main subjects for his teaching: conduct, culture, loyalty and good faith. Of the importance of ritual in government he said . . .

If one can govern a country by ritual and deference, there is no more to be said; but if one cannot govern a country by ritual and deference, then what has one to do with ritual?

Three Main Principles

Confucianists were concerned with the balance between individual integrity and social harmony. So there are three main principles . . .

1) **Jen**, human-heartedness (goodness, proper being).
2) **Li**, etiquette (propriety, rules).
3) **Chih**, righteousness (proper behaviour).

> To achieve Jen one must behave properly in all human relationships, but particularly within the five that are stipulated in traditional culture.

1) Between father and son.	2) Between ruler and minister.	3) Between elder and younger brother.	4) Between husband and wife.	5) Between friend and friend.

> You will notice that women are only mentioned once in these important relationships!

Negative and Positive Jen

So the way of Jen is to practise chung and shu.

How to Behave

Behaviour should be regulated by "oughtness" or what ought to be done in a particular situation. This was later described as "the principle of applying a measuring square", or working out what ought to be done by applying the rules and sticking to them.

Moral excellence, then, was expressed by the combination of right behaviour, right approach and integrity, exemplified in the person of the **Chun-Tzu** (or gentleman). Confucius himself is, of course, the ultimate model for all of these approaches and therein lies the reason for his endurance.

Mencius

Confucius' great disciple **Mencius** (371–289 B.C.) developed and codified the sage's ideas, as well as trying to explain why man should act in the right way.

The central question was precisely the nature of human nature: was it good, bad or indifferent, or all three? Mencius said there were three theories besides his own.
1) That all men are good and bad.
2) That men are neither good nor bad.
3) That some are good and some are bad.

Mencius, being a bit of an optimist, claimed that we are all born with a capacity for goodness, what he called the "four beginnings". He argued that we are all born with a sense of **Jen** (humanity), **I** (righteousness), **Li** (propriety), and **Chih** (wisdom). If these innate properties are allowed to grow normally they will develop into the four constant virtues. Just as right behaviour in human relationships is the basis of all ethics, so proper behaviour is the hallmark of a good citizen and a moral state. This is why a ruler should be a gentleman and a sage, rather like Plato's philosopher King. Indeed, if a ruler does not rule wisely and morally, the people have a right to overthrow him.

This radical idea only appeared in the West in the 17th and 18th centuries.

Mencius was bandied about in the revolutions of this century in China, particularly when he said . . .

The people are the most important element in a state, the spirits of the land and the grain are secondary, and the sovereign is the least.

For Mencius, family life was the proper way to implement Jen. For a proper state to operate, this meant the fair distribution of land, in what he called the "well-field" system. Like other aspects of Chinese philosophy, this embodied a rational, unitary and socially cohesive way of running things. It wasn't always followed, of course.

Some say that Mencius extended the teachings of Confucius on the self-cultivation of the individual outwards to the cultivation of all.

Others say that he was far too much of an idealist.

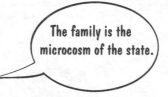

The family is the microcosm of the state.

Like Confucius, he supported **ritual**, the **family**, and the idea of the **Golden Mean**.

The School of Names

Put simply, these philosophers were interested in the meaning of names. Confucius called it the "rectification of names", by which he meant getting it right when giving something a name. (Calling a spade a spade?) In other words, the proper description and analysis of things is necessary in order to avoid falsehood and illusion. The question is of the relationship between **Ming** (the name) and **Shih** (the actuality).

The allusive nature of the Chinese language represented a serious philosophical problem.

They even used the example of

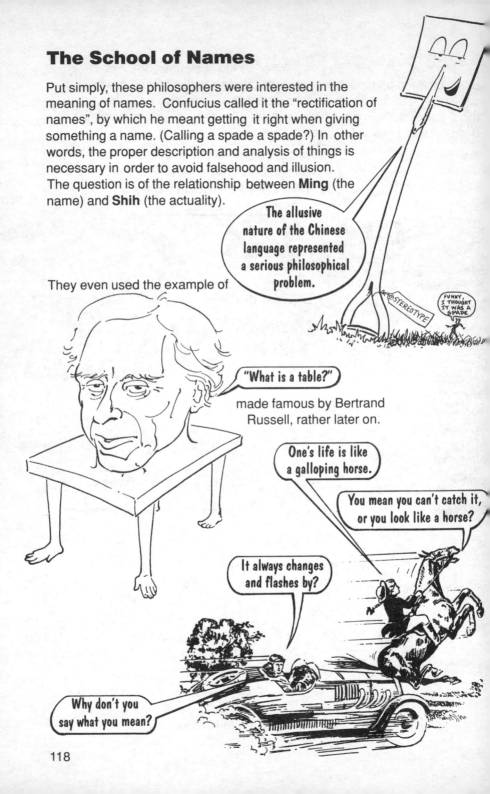

STEREOTYPE

FUNNY, I THOUGHT IT WAS A SPADE

"What is a table?"

made famous by Bertrand Russell, rather later on.

One's life is like a galloping horse.

You mean you can't catch it, or you look like a horse?

It always changes and flashes by?

Why don't you say what you mean?

The Problem of Universals

The debates within the **School of Names** were sometimes just complex and tricky interpretations of the way things mean (**sophistry**, it came to be called by the Greeks). The important philosophical point to it all was the nature of **universals**, or how language describes things.

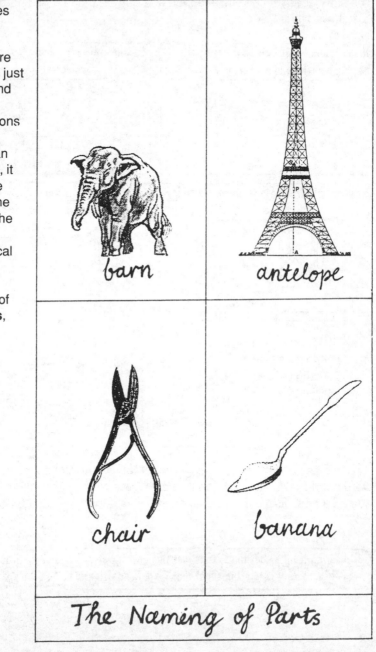

barn

antelope

chair

banana

The Naming of Parts

One of the more famous members of the Names school was **Kung-sun Lung** (4th century B.C.), who wrote the famous "White Horse Discourse". The story goes that he was stopped at a border and told that horses were not allowed in.

It comes as no surprise to discover that many in the School of Names were lawyers who could argue that black was white. Confucius himself had a healthy dislike of legal things and was quoted as saying . . .

The Mohist School

Based on the work of **Mo-Tzu** (c. 479–381 B.C.), and on the book of the same name, this school was anti-Confucian and anti-tradition. Mo criticized Confucius' love of ritual and music from the standpoint of the lower classes, who were excluded from such noble goings on. It is said that Mo-Tzu represented the class of knights (**Hseih**) who did the fighting rather than the talking, and were therefore rather more practical about institutions and rituals.

In the *Mo-Tzu* itself, nine chapters are devoted to the tactics of fighting and defence techniques.

But we did not approve of aggressive wars.

The **Mohist** school had a practical and utilitarian approach, but it did speak of an all-embracing love which was meant to be the guiding principle of all action.

Everyone should be treated with the same universal love, but must obey the rules.

Anti-Confucius

Mo-Tzu said that Confucius got it all wrong on four major counts.
1) The Confucianists did not believe in spirits or gods, which would displease them.
2) The Confucianists believed that one should mourn parents for three years, which wasted everybody's time and energy.
3) They liked music which also wasted everybody's time.
4) Confucianists seemed to believe in a predetermined fate, which made everybody passive and lazy.

Mo-Tzu also didn't think much of all the learning and ritual that Confucianists went in for.

> There isn't time for all that sort of thing, especially when the rice harvest has to be got in.

His was a practical, all-embracing, hearty sort of "let's all get on with it" philosophy.

Mohist Dialectics

The Mohists' utilitarian view of the world led them to defend commonsense and to dismiss most philosophical speculation. They disliked the Taoists in particular for their other-worldliness and their disdain for practical knowledge.

Their idea of all-embracing love sounds very nice, but how are you supposed to love everybody?

Even the person who robs you?

Oddly enough, the Mohists were very keen on the **dialectic** as a means of reasoning and rebutting their opponents' arguments. It seems odd because the dialectic (thesis-antithesis-synthesis) is often associated in philosophy with difficult, obscure and theoretical approaches to the world. So we can say the Mohists provided quite a complex way of arguing for straightforward commonsense and utilitarian approaches.

Of the benefits, choose the greatest. Of the harms, choose the slightest.

The Fa Chia, or Legalist School

Whereas Confucius argued that good government was based on tradition, ritual and loyalty, the **Legalist School**, as its name suggests, argued for the rule of law. They did not believe, like many of the other philosophers, that a natural moral law would take care of how people should behave, but rather that a fixed code of law had to be drawn up and enforced. **Han-Tzu** (280–233 B.C.) was one of the reformers who belonged to this school of modernizers.

We are realists and do not believe in man's natural goodness, rather in the practical enforcement of laws drawn up by the necessary authorities.

THE CARROT

THE STICK

THE LAWS

Because the old order was falling apart at this time, a new, centralized order was necessary. We came up with the "two handles" of reward and punishment.

The Legalists were not just concerned with the law, however, but more with the theory of how to rule. They were in fact early political theorists, and perhaps the best comparison is with Machiavelli's realism.

We did not look to the gods or to the ancients and were centrally concerned with how to organise the state and exercise power.

This realism may not seem so revolutionary, but in a culture where tradition was everything, it was actually very radical.

As conditions in the world change, different principles are practised.

The School of Tao

The sixth school in the original group derived from Ssu-ma Ch'ien's description was the Taoist school or the **Tao Te-Chia**, the school of the Way and its Power. Tao is more than just a school of philosophy. It is one of the basics of Chinese culture (and a religion!). According to tradition, the writings of **Lao-Tzu** are the oldest philosophical works of the Chinese canon, but this may be inaccurate. The *Tao Te Ching* (the *Way of the Power*), next to the Confucian *Analects*, is the most famous work of Chinese philosophy. The *Tao Te Ching*, supposedly written by Lao-Tzu in one night, is the most aphoristic and least down-to-earth book in the early tradition.

The Tao that can be spoken of is not the real Tao. The name that can be named is not the true name.

The Way

Tao actually means the "Way" or the Universal Path. It is the force that governs the Universe. Or as the *Tao Te Ching* puts it:

The Tao gives birth to the One;
The One gives birth to the Two;

The Two gives birth to the Three;
The Three gives birth to all things.

This is clearly a much more abstract approach than many of the other schools. The central idea of Tao is a terribly slippery one, over which there is rather a lot of debate. To see Tao as a force, a power (**Te** means power) and a way of relating to it is perhaps the clearest approximation.

Enough birth, already.

The essential way of the Tao is that it is not nameable.

The Tao represents the ultimate reality, which cannot be described, but which is the origin of all things.

The Unnameable is the beginning of Heaven and Earth.

Only through relating to the power of Tao, in harmony with the forces of nature, can one's Te be achieved.

Wu-Wei

Liu Hsin said that the Taoists came from the hermits. Confucius said they were **Yin Che**, "those who obscure themselves". . .

Which doesn't sound very complimentary.

We Taoists didn't think too much of Confucius trying to make the world a better place.

Because of their position on the forces of nature and the ultimately unchanging reality that lay behind all change, the Taoists generally wanted to escape from the world, not interfere with it. Lao-Tzu tells us . . .

The conquest of the world comes invariably from doing nothing.

This principle of "letting be" they called **Wu-Wei**.

The Power of Te

Confucianists said that the Taoists were just selfish, or "each one for himself". One of the early Taoists, **Yang Chu**, is supposed to have said that he wouldn't have exchanged ruling the world for one hair off his back, which seems a little bit extreme. Their basic argument is that one should despise things and value life, which seems more reasonable.

As Yang Chu put it . . .

Our life is our own possession, and its benefit to us is very great.

Taoists aimed at a life of simplicity and harmony with Tao, not being ruled by intellect, but by a natural power, or Te.

To preserve self, Taoists argued, the proper way was to regulate one's behaviour according to the underlying rules of nature. Lao-Tzu summed it all up.

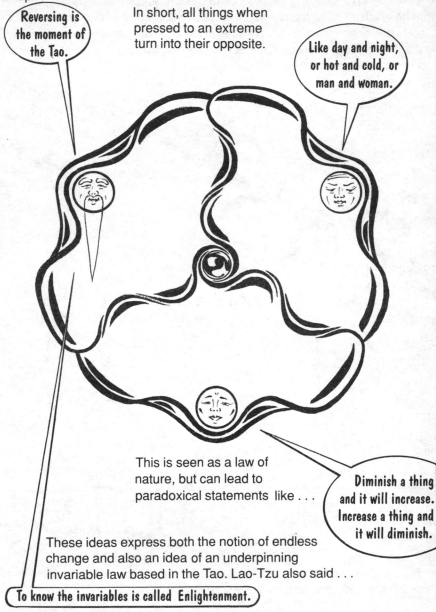

Reversing is the moment of the Tao.

In short, all things when pressed to an extreme turn into their opposite.

Like day and night, or hot and cold, or man and woman.

This is seen as a law of nature, but can lead to paradoxical statements like . . .

Diminish a thing and it will increase. Increase a thing and it will diminish.

These ideas express both the notion of endless change and also an idea of an underpinning invariable law based in the Tao. Lao-Tzu also said . . .

To know the invariables is called Enlightenment.

So true knowledge is knowing the basis of all things, the way of the Tao.

One of the main themes of Taoism is the notion of Wu-Wei, or "non- action".

It is a methodical calmness in which the least necessary action is taken.

Perhaps "not over-doing it" would be a modern colloquial translation.

Put like this, you can see how this approach appealed to Beatniks in the West.

Or "Let it be", as the Beatles put it.

To follow the way of the Tao, to exercise the power of the Tao (the Te) is to practise Wu-Wei.

Tao and Politics

Did Lao-Tzu exist and live in the sixth century B.C.? Did he write the book bearing his name in the one night before he "went West"? We have to exercise Wu-Wei here and just look at the book of the name and accept its existence without questioning the history too much. As Lao-Tzu said . . .

To know how to be content is to avoid humiliation; to know where to stop is to avoid injury.

Lao-Tzu's political theory was based on this premise as well.

A good ruler should do as little as possible and leave the people to get on with what they can do, and want to do.

This sounds like modern New Right politics in which the state is supposed to interfere as little as possible.

Chuang-Tzu

After Lao-Tzu (which also means Old Master),
there were others who developed Taoist
philosophy. **Chuang-Tzu** (369–286 B.C.) was
another great exponent of Taoism and
reputedly lived as a hermit.

> I prefer the enjoyment
> of my own free will.

The text that bears his name, the
Chuang-Tzu, undoubtedly written
much later by his disciples,
tells us this sort of thing.
Chuang-Tzu was all for living
according to nature, avoiding
artificiality and government of any
sort, and following the way of the
Tao as the unity of opposites.
He was apparently very famous
in his own time and turned down
any offers of running things.

> Those Taoists aren't much better than
> anarchists, even if they haven't been
> invented yet.

Nature and Knowledge

Taoism might be seen as just accepting the way the world is, living by its rules and trying to avoid any difficulties. A Confucian cynic might say that the fantastic allegories and paradoxical sayings of the Taoists didn't add up to anything other than the avoidance of complex realities. Take Chuang-Tzu's argument about the nature of different abilities in things. He says . . .

The duck's legs are short, but if we try to lengthen them, the duck will feel pain.

That is probably true, but is it a philosophy for understanding the Universe?

Actually, Chuang-Tzu is making an important point that nature and knowledge are specific to specific things, and happiness comes from being true to your proper nature, or Te.

Happiness of the Sage

The Taoists were very interested in ways of achieving absolute happiness, of harmony with one's Te, or innate nature. For example, there is discussion in the *Chuang-Tzu* on death, on the fear and anxiety that accompany it.

If one properly understands the natural order of things, of which death is a part . . .

. . . then fear and mourning will no longer be necessary.

One can "disperse emotion with reason".

In Western philosophy, this would accord with Spinoza's views on reason's control of emotions.

A passion dissolves when I can form a clear, distinct idea of it.

Baruch de Spinoza

So the ultimate Tao sage is one who has transcended emotion, worldly attachments and distractions and is at one with the Tao, the nameless and the nothingness.

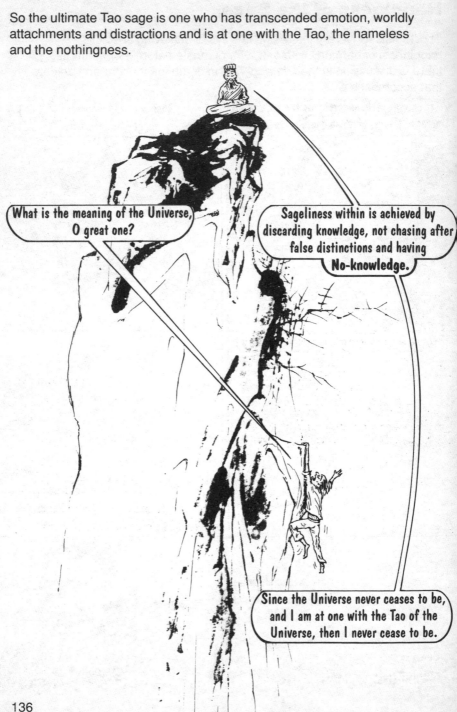

What is the meaning of the Universe, O great one?

Sageliness within is achieved by discarding knowledge, not chasing after false distinctions and having No-knowledge.

Since the Universe never ceases to be, and I am at one with the Tao of the Universe, then I never cease to be.

By the time of the two historians, Ssu-ma Ch'ien (died 110 B.C) and Liu Hsin (46 B.C.–A.D. 23), there was an increasing eclecticism within Chinese philosophy. Different kinds of approaches were lifted from each school. The **Great Appendix to the Yi** (the **Yi Wen Chih** or "Treatise on Literature" derived from Liu Hsin), puts it like this . . .

In the world there is one purpose, but there are a hundred ideas about it; there is a single goal, but the paths toward it differ.

This very much represents the eclectic spirit of Chinese philosophy. Despite their dismissal of each other, Confucianism and Taoism share that general approach of "Sageliness within and Kingliness without".

Buddhism in China

Buddhism, which began in India with Siddhartha Gautama, the Enlightened One, then spread throughout the East. A major influence in China, Tibet, South East Asia and Japan, yet in India itself, Buddhism almost completely disappeared.

It is a particular mystery why this alien religion managed to implant itself in China, in a culture that was practical, secular and not very fond of foreign things.

The Buddhist ideas of no-self, withdrawal from the world and self- liberation seem to be the very opposite of Confucian social thinking.

Perhaps the Chinese were bored with being practical and actually wanted a bit of spiritual relief?

How Buddhism Arrived in China

Buddhist ideas probably filtered into China via the silk route and the channels of trade, but the opposition to them was official, cultural and powerful. Perhaps because the officials championed Confucianism and Taoism, the people took to the Buddhist message of liberation.

The condition of the Chinese peasantry was seriously grim.

Something that promised definite release would seem attractive.

Whatever the reasons, the introduction of Buddhism to China was a "cultural revolution" with a long-term impact.

The other-worldliness of Taoism may also explain the reception of Buddhism. Both have in common a search for universal Enlightenment and a rejection of worldly ties.

Different versions of Buddhism had developed in India, particularly the **Hinayana** (small vehicle) and **Mahayana** (great vehicle). So, in China too, we find different schools: the two most influential were **Ch'an** (Zen) and the **Middle Path**. The others were:

Chinese Buddhist Schools	
School	*Prominent Figure*
Three Treatises (San-lun) or Middle Doctrine	Chi-tsang (549–623)
Consciousness Only or Mere Ideation	Hsüan-tsang (596–664)
T'ien-T'ai (Fa-hua) or Lotus School	Chih-k'ai (538–597)
Hua-yen or Wreath School	Fa-tsang (643–712)
Ch'an	Bodhidharma (fl. 460–534)

Taoists and Confucianists, at various points, claimed that Buddhism really started in China. One story is that Lao-Tzu, after he "went West", taught the Buddha and started the whole thing.

Go West, old man.

"Going West" is a polite way of saying "kicking the bucket".

Indian Missionaries

In fact, Buddhism was brought to China by various Indian missionaries. Chinese scholars who visited India also brought back ideas and texts which were then translated. It is thought that the influence of Buddhism began during the reign of **Emperor Ming** (A.D. 58–75), but was seen as rather occultish. During the third and fourth centuries, more and more Buddhist texts were translated and their influence grew, possibly as a result of the political turmoil of the times. **Kumarajiva** (343–413), who introduced the *Madhyamika Sastra*, was so influential that he was held captive at the court and developed his ideas whilst translating texts.

My disciples **Seng-Chao** and **Tao-Sheng** were also important in developing Chinese Buddhism.

Ch'an Buddhism

Bodhidharma (460–534) brought in Ch'an (Zen) which later became important in Japan. Ch'an emphasized meditation and study.

Concentrate on understanding the essence of things at the present moment and grasping reality directly.

It is anti-philosophical by not relying on words or conceptual understanding. They studied **Koans**, which are like little riddles, to point you at the nature of ultimate reality.

How do you get rid of ignorance?

Karma or Yeh

The idea of karma, translated into Chinese as **Yeh**, is still central in Chinese Buddhism, as is the idea that the individual is responsible for actions that produce consequences.

The way out is to identify with the Universal Mind.

The overlap with the Taoist idea of the eternal forces of nature and the Universe is clear.

Non-attachment is a common thread in both approaches.

The Mahayana school of Buddhism believes in showing compassion to all things and people. Its more egalitarian approach perhaps explains why it took off in repressive Chinese society.

The ignorance which leads the mind to seek the world, which is illusory, is called **Wu-Ming**, from the Sanskrit, **Avidya**. The aim is to achieve nirvana or Enlightenment. Nirvana is similar to the Taoist notion of no-self blending with the forces of the Universe. But it also means clicking in with the **Universal Mind**.

What Buddhism brought to Chinese philosophy was the idea of the Universal Mind.

GUAN YIN
(CHINESE FORM OF BODHISATTVA AVALOKITESVARA)

Buddhism gave a particular reading to the abstract Taoist notions of the forces of the Universe and turned no-self into mind.

Japanese Buddhism

The introduction of Buddhism to Japan in the 6th century A.D. was the crucial step in the development of Japanese philosophy. This led eventually to the formation of the Japanese form of **Zen** Buddhism, which epitomizes the special character of the Japanese Way.

There are many other philosophies in Japanese history, but none which better conveys the essence of Japanese thought than Zen.

What is Zen?

Zen is so unique that it puts the uninitiated out of their wits.

One master, when asked the nature of Zen, said . . .

I raise my eyebrows, I move my eyes.

He meant that the nature of Zen is both ordinary and extraordinary and can be conveyed in almost anything.

Zen is the attempt to fathom the mysterious nature of things and beings.

Zen is the art of living Zen.

It also permeates the Samurai Warrior code of **Bushido**.

Key Zen Ideas

The many different forms of Buddhism all seek after Enlightenment, the fundamental idea of no-self and liberation from the world. Debates about what constitutes nirvana are irrelevant to the Ch'an (Zen) school's answer that it is inexpressible.

Attempting to define it means that you fall into the "net of words" wherein nothing can be said.

Zen took over from Ch'an certain key ideas, but Zen thought is a long way from original Buddhist principles.

Its key ideas are . . .

1) Genuine Enlightenment is **instantaneous**. Preparation may be necessary, but true realization is a total experience.

2) Zen involves action through non-action, working towards a result in which no-self is exercised.

3) Enlightenment and ordinary experience are related, but scriptures, texts and theory do not provide the path to nirvana.

4) A true sage lives in every man and in all things. One does not have to retreat to the mountains to find Enlightenment.

These ideas are radical, difficult and very different to mainstream Buddhism or Japan's aboriginal, animistic religion of **Shintoism**.

Is Zen a Philosophy?

If philosophy in its broadest sense is understanding the world we live in, then Zen philosophy is clearly that. In terms of Western logic, however, it isn't "properly" philosophy. Japanese ways of thinking about the world are concerned with the clarity and precision of images, rather than with formal logic. Japanese philosophy can be seen in its art, its calligraphy, its ritual, in the order and interconnectedness of its culture. This is its secret.

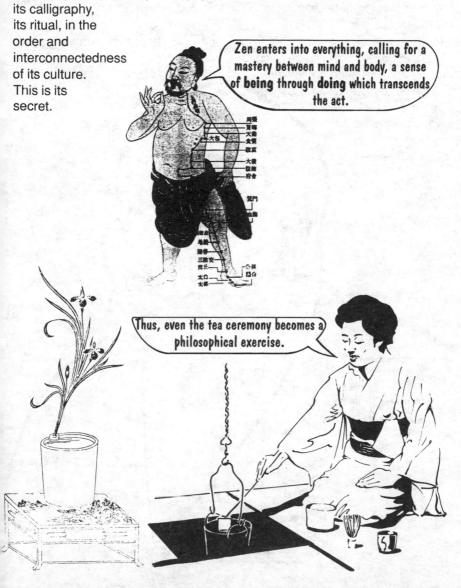

Zen enters into everything, calling for a mastery between mind and body, a sense of **being** through **doing** which transcends the act.

Thus, even the tea ceremony becomes a philosophical exercise.

Dogen, Zen Master

The most famous exponent of Zen in Japan is **Dogen** (1200–53). His work *Shobogenzo* (*Treasury of the True Dharma Eye*) is the first Buddhist text written in Japanese, rather than classical Chinese. It is said to be the first truly philosophical work in Japan and is certainly difficult. Dogen strongly urged meditation. The word Zen ultimately derives from the Sanskrit for meditation, which Dogen called **Zazen** (seated meditation).

Meditation leads to the intuitive experience which transcends ordinary reality. It can be described as finding one's true nature. One aims for the losing of "body-mind" to achieve a non-conceptual awareness. The impermanence of the world is emphasized by Dogen.

The illusion of the ego is a fabrication, and only by accepting this do we move along the Buddha Way.

Impermanence is truly the reality right in front of our eyes.

Dogen also emphasizes the Buddha-nature or enlightened nature of the whole world.

Dogen

Buddha-nature is that "nothingness" that we must recognize as the essential emptiness of all things. Things do not have a meaning in themselves, but only in relation to other things.

For Westerners obsessed with the classification of material things, this is a truly radical idea. Dogen goes on to say . . .

Buddha-nature is vast emptiness, open, clear and bright.

The impermanence of things also led Dogen to speculate about the nature of Time itself. The past, the present and the future are combined in the moments of Enlightenment.

Neo-Confucianism in China

After a long period of wars and civil disarray, China was reunited in 589 under the **Sui** dynasty, and with this came a revival of Confucianism. For some time, the Confucianists had attacked the Buddhists for their escapism and anti-social attitudes. The restored Imperial Court also sought to restore Confucianism to its central role in Chinese cultural life.

We returned to the original Confucian texts, reinterpreted in terms of the new situation.

This was **Neo-Confucianism**, which remained central to Chinese thought until the revolutions of the 20th century.

The famous examination system for the election of officials was also reintroduced in 622 with the Confucian classics as its basis.

The underlying pattern of Chinese culture, based on family, agriculture and social relations, simply reasserted itself.

Under the **Tang** dynasty (618–906), a centralized and powerful court ruled supreme once again, and a pair of brothers, both philosophers, emerged to rethink Confucianism. **Han Yu** (768–824) and **Li Ao** (died 844) set about putting the philosophical house in order. Li Ao, in an essay *On the Restoration of Nature*, summed up the superior Confucian approach.

Alas, though writings dealing with nature and Destiny are still preserved, none of the scholars understands them, and therefore they all plunge into Taoism and Buddhism.

Neo-Confucianism looked for happiness in the old Confucian ideas of morals, rituals and institutions.

One of the central philosophical debates was between **Li** and **Ch'i**.

Let's see . . .

What is the relationship between the two?

Ch'i, The Great Harmony

The philosopher **Chang Tsai** (1020–77) emphasized the importance of **Ch'i** in his *Cheng Meng*, or

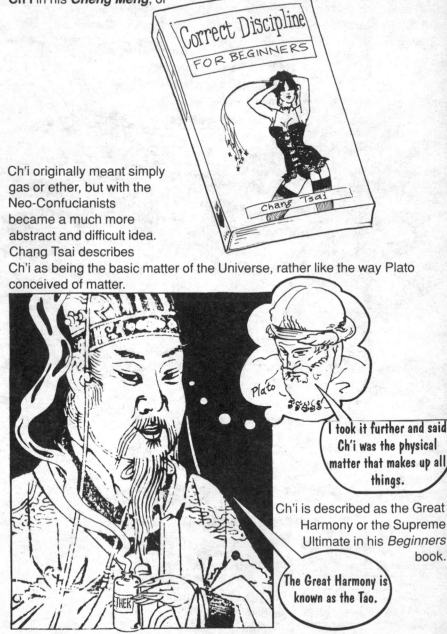

Ch'i originally meant simply gas or ether, but with the Neo-Confucianists became a much more abstract and difficult idea. Chang Tsai describes Ch'i as being the basic matter of the Universe, rather like the way Plato conceived of matter.

Plato

I took it further and said Ch'i was the physical matter that makes up all things.

Ch'i is described as the Great Harmony or the Supreme Ultimate in his *Beginners* book.

The Great Harmony is known as the Tao.

Ch'i and Social Morality

Although it may not seem obvious, Chang Tsai was trying to get away from Taoist and Buddhist ideas of non-being, and back to a position where social morality was important. If everything was simply nothingness, then it was difficult to argue for social ethics. Nihilism could be just as sensible. Therefore he said . . .

If one knows the Void is the Ch'i, one knows that there is no Wu (non-being).

He argued that the Void was not an absolute vacuum, that the Ch'i was dispersed in a way that was not visible.

Chang Tsai therefore gave back to Confucianism a philosophical basis for social morality, which was an important thing to do.

One very famous passage from the *Cheng Meng* became known as the "Western Inscription", because Chang Tsai had it up on the Western wall of his study:

Since all things in the Universe are constituted of Ch'i,
therefore men and all other things are but part of our great body...
I live, I serve the Universal parents and when death comes
I rest.

Neo-Confucianists were fond of this because it clearly distinguished the Confucian approach from the Buddhist and Taoist.

The Form of Li

The nature of **Li** and **Ch'i** is very similar to the Western philosophical debate about the form and matter of things found in Plato and Aristotle.

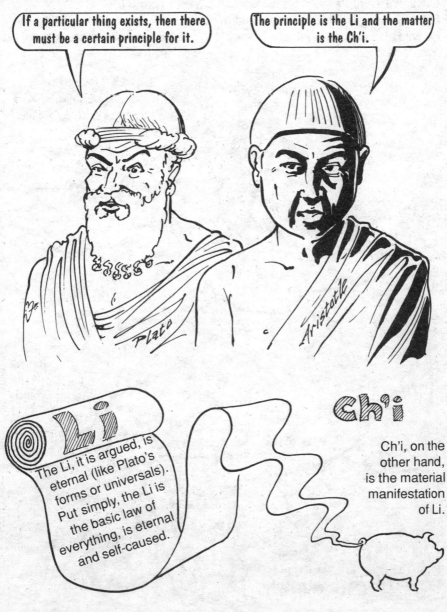

If a particular thing exists, then there must be a certain principle for it.

The principle is the Li and the matter is the Ch'i.

Plato

Aristotle

Li

The Li, it is argued, is eternal (like Plato's forms or universals). Put simply, the Li is the basic law of everything, is eternal and self-caused.

ch'i

Ch'i, on the other hand, is the material manifestation of Li.

The Two Schools

Brothers seemed to play quite an important role in Neo-Confucianism. Another pair, known as the Ch'eng Masters, started what became known as the Two Schools. **Ch'eng Yi** (1033–1108) inaugurated the **School of Laws or Principles** and his big brother **Ch'eng Hao** (1032–1085) the **School of Mind**. Ch'eng Yi said that the Great Ultimate was the T'ai Chi. He was also concerned about shapes. Li, he said, was above shapes, as was Tao. This meant that Li was logically prior to Ch'i.

What this means is that the principle of a horse exists before the horse itself.

But the nature of Li is that it naturally manifests itself. Horse has its own principle.

And all this comes about because Ch'i combines with the energies of Yin and Yang and produces matter.

Chu-Tzu

The School of Laws was completed by Chu-Hsi, also known as **Chu-Tzu** (1130–1200), called the St. Thomas Aquinas of China. This means he produced a complete metaphysical system of philosophy that was rather scholastic. His recorded sayings run to about 140 books, besides commentaries on the famous *Four Books* which became the main texts used in state examinations.

The four books were

The Analects

The Mencius

The Doctrine of the Mean

Ta Hsueh (Great Learning)

From 1313, under Emperor Jen-Tsung, until the abolition of the state examinations in 1905, my way of interpreting things was supreme.

So, what kind of philosophy did Chu-Tzu put forward?

Chu-Tzu synthesized the basic doctrines of the Confucian philosophers into a coherent unity and clarified the Li and Ch'i debate. "For everything there is a Li, which makes it what it ought to be, or a thing is a concrete instance of its Li." At the same time, there must be an ultimate standard for the whole Universe, which embraces all Li. This is called the Supreme Ultimate or the T'ai Chi. (We in the West usually put God in here to explain things.)

When called upon to explain the connection between the Supreme Ultimate, the Li and the Ch'i, Chu-Tzu used a metaphor about the moon.

It is like the moon shining in the heavens, of which, though it is reflected in rivers and lakes and thus is everywhere visible, we would not therefore say that it is divided.

Neo-Confucian Politics

In terms of politics, Chu-Tzu proposed all of the Confucian values – a philosopher-sage as ruler and a people who lived a life of virtue. Man, he argued, had the Great Ultimate within him. It was a matter of bringing it out through self-cultivation and the investigation of things. Again, Chu-Tzu sounds like Plato, with a collective approach much like Plato's Republic in which wisdom and order are put above individuality and self-expression.

No wonder then that your philosophy met with official approval.

Actually, I myself thought that proper government had not often been exercised, and the principle or Li of good government was still waiting to be expressed.

The School of Mind

The School of Mind begun by Ch'eng Hao was completed by **Lu Chu-Yuan** (1139–93) and **Wang Shou-Jen** (1472–1529). Lu Chu-Yuan is supposed to have had a sudden enlightenment and said . . .

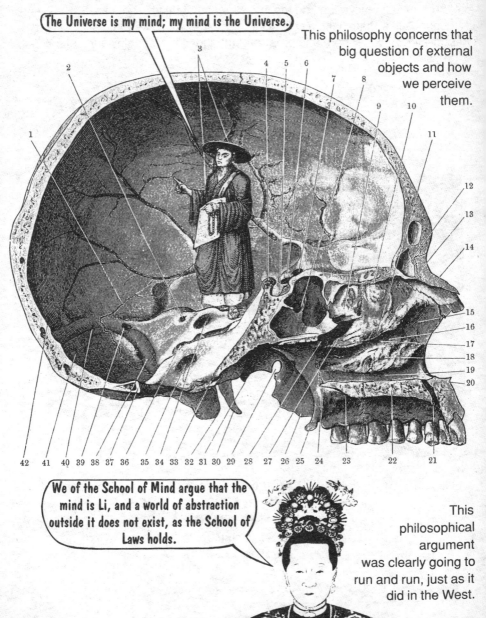

The Universe is my mind; my mind is the Universe.

This philosophy concerns that big question of external objects and how we perceive them.

We of the School of Mind argue that the mind is Li, and a world of abstraction outside it does not exist, as the School of Laws holds.

This philosophical argument was clearly going to run and run, just as it did in the West.

Wang Shou-Jen's argument for intuitive knowledge was based on the Unity of Thought and Action. He criticized the Taoists and the Buddhists for their escapism and their refusal to think about practical human relations. He stressed that very Chinese, and Eastern, idea of the unity and interconnectedness of all things.

He was followed by the **Empirical School** which also advocated a return to Confucius and Mencius. **Tai Chen** (1723–77) was the greatest exponent of this approach, which sought to re-establish a more practical philosophy.

All Chinese philosophy can be seen as a battle between the practicality of Confucius and the mysticism of Taoism.

What about Buddhism?

It pretended to be both, whilst providing an escape from the social realities of familial society.

Modern China

At the turn of this century, in 1898, there was a reform movement in China against the inept **Manchu** governments and the dire influence of Europe.

Reform meant going back to the classics.

One leading philosopher, **K'ang Yu-Wei** (1858–1927), argued the case that Confucius had really been a reformer, not a conservative.

This could be shown in his philosophy.

The "Hundred Days of Reform" got off to a good start but rapidly ran out of steam. Many people, including the philosopher **T'an Ssu-Tung** (1837–1909), were executed.

I had attempted to synthesize the Mencian idea of love with modern physics and chemistry. My quest for the new age of Great Unity cost me my head.

Influences from the West were few and far between, but the American pragmatist philosopher, **John Dewey** (1859–1952) and the British logician, **Bertrand Russell** (1872–1970) went to Peking in 1919–20 to deliver lectures at the University. There is not much sign that they radically altered traditional Chinese philosophy.

Knowledge is an instrument for action, not contemplation.

I have devised a theory about the nature of facts which I call "logical atomism".

What the Chinese made of Dewey's pragmatic notion of truth and Bertrand Russell's rampant individualism is anybody's guess.

Yen-Fu (1853–1920) was the greatest authority on Western thought at the turn of the century, and translated a number of Western classics.

Because I translated them into classical Chinese they were treated with great respect and very widely read.

Strangely, he recommended the British sociologist **Herbert Spencer** (1820–1903) as the greatest Western philosopher of all time. Spencer certainly was an influential social philosopher in his time, and this suggests that Yen-Fu was attracted to him because of Chinese practical concerns with social reform. Western philosophy was naturally read through the grid of Eastern philosophy.

Marxist Maoism

Marxism was the most potent form of Western thinking in China, and inspired social reform, particularly in the 1930s and 1940s, which led to the Great Revolution. But a peculiarly Chinese version of Marxism came to be officially embraced, that of **Maoism**. If you look carefully, you can see that Maoism is actually an eclectic 20th century version of Neo-Confucianism.

Are you saying Mao's Cultural Revolution was a Neo-Confucian experiment?

Not as strange as it sounds if you consider the radical legacies of traditional Chinese philosophy.

I always argued that the people had a right to be governed properly and that a true ruler would be a sage.

I played heavily on these ideas and presented myself as the Great Teacher, consciously echoing Confucius.

On Contradiction

Mao Tse-Tung (1893–1976) put himself forward as a philosopher and justified his policies by reference to dialectical thinking. His famous essay *On Contradiction* (1937) appears to be a classic statement of Marxism-Leninism-Maoism, but it echoes classical Chinese philosophy in interesting ways.

Contradictions exist in all developmental processes . . .

Maybe so, but the Marxist theory of knowledge is completely and qualitatively different.

Well, it sounds like a version of Taoism to me.

Not Taoism, **Maoism**, you revisionist!

Mao's view of a hierarchy of contradictions, interpenetrating one another, sounds remarkably like the ideas of the complementarity of Yin and Yang.

Maoism is the way of social reform which Chinese radicals chose to come to terms with the West and integrate modernization into Chinese thought. Mao insisted that one had to deal with the particular and the concrete in thought, not just with theoretical abstractions. His emphasis on real historical conditions and the importance of practice, not theory, sounds very materialist but can also be understood as a form of Zen in reverse.

Mao says...

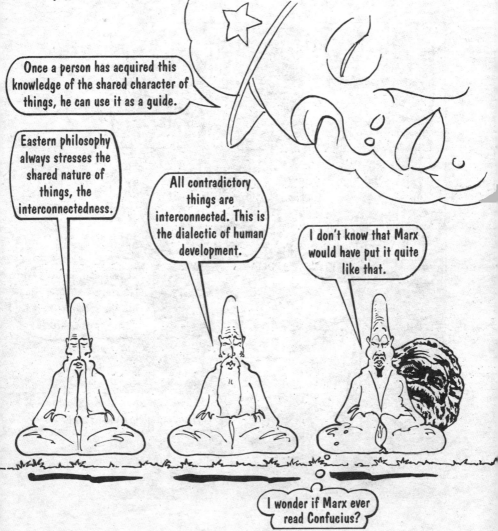

169

Ancient or Postmodern?

Chinese philosophy seemed to be old when it started. Confucius was always referring to traditions that went back centuries, and upholding them as examples to be followed. Some 2,500 years later, many of the same themes are present.

Mao Tse-Tung and Western philosophy have made major inroads into Chinese tradition.

But even now, in the post-Mao era, we are grappling with the social ideas that derive from Confucius.

And we have to do it in the context of a postmodern globalized world economy . . .

The late 20th century is characterized by the information superhighway and a global free market economy. The world has never seemed so homogeneous, with all of its societies mutually influenced by the same economic and cultural patterns.

Western philosophy, science and technology have been crucial in installing a universal "mass media" order, but this does not settle the question of whether Western or Eastern cultures are better equipped to grapple with "hyperreality".

There are advantages to traditional Eastern philosophies . . .

For instance, in the application of Indian logic to computerology.

Or take Japan, the supreme model of postmodern success, with its unique amalgam of tradition, hi-tech and systems management . . .

But the practice of traditional Buddhism is in decline among younger Japanese . . .

Beyond East and West?

Postmodernity has also provoked a fundamentalist reaction in the East, with the threat to traditional cultures being met by "hyper"-traditionalism. Yet, we have seen how Eastern attitudes of reverence for continuity and cosmic unity are perfectly compatible with acceptance of impermanence, illusion and liberation from the ego falsehood. Eastern thinking has found ways of overcoming the apparent contradiction between change and sameness, and this may be its remedial contribution to moderating the intellectual arrogance and destructive short-sightedness of Western cultures.

Postscript

May the noble-minded scholars instead of cherishing ill-feeling kindly correct whatever errors have been committed through the dullness of my intellect in the way of wrong interpretations and misstatements.
Hemacandra

THE AUTHOR, RICHARD OSBORNE, WAS GOING TO BE A PROFESSIONAL FOOTBALLER. INSTEAD HE BECAME SENIOR LECTURER AT LONDON GUILDHALL UNIVERSITY. HE HAS LECTURED IN SYDNEY & LONDON & IS THE AUTHOR OF THE "RADICAL PHILOSOPHY READER" & OF THE FORTHCOMING "SOCIOLOGY FOR BEGINNERS"

THE ILLUSTRATOR, BORIN VAN LOON, HAS TOILED LONG INTO THE NIGHT ON BEGINNERS BOOKS, AMONGST THEM "DARWIN", "GENETICS" & "BUDDHA". HE HAS CONTRIBUTED A MURAL ON DNA (IN "BEGINNERS" STYLE) TO THE "HEALTH MATTERS" GALLERY IN THE SCIENCE MUSEUM, LONDON.

Bibliography

Getting into Eastern Philosophy is not an easy task, partly because of the overlap between religion and philosophy that we discussed earlier. There are, however, some recent works that attempt to provide an overview.

This very recent interest is a product of the last ten years. Going back to the Classics themselves is always a good start, but they are often difficult to understand without any prior knowledge.

General Reading
These texts are all generally accessible to the non-philosopher and cover historical background as well as the philosophy.
Eberhard, W., **Conquerors and Rulers**. Leiden: E.J.Brill 1952
Hackett, S.C., **Oriental Philosophy: A Westerner's Guide to Eastern Thought**. Madison: University of Wisconsin Press 1979
Hinnells, J.R., **A Handbook of Living Religions**. London: Penguin 1984
Hope, J. & Van Loon, B., **Buddha for Beginners**. Cambridge: Icon Books 1994
Legge, J., **The Chinese Classics Vol.1**. Hong Kong: 1861.
Sastri, P.D., **The Essentials of Eastern Philosophy**. 1928 (Difficult to get hold of — should be reprinted.)
Schwartz, B., **The World of Thought in Ancient China**. Cambridge, Mass: Harvard University Press 1985
Sen, K.M., **Hinduism**. London: Penguin 1991
Smart, N., **The World's Religions**. Cambridge University Press 1989
Solomon, R.C. & Higgins, K.M., **World Philosophy — a Text with Readings**. McGraw-Hill 1995 (Short introduction to many world philosophies with readings.)
Cooper, D.E., **World Philosophies**. Blackwell 1995 (Wide overview at more difficult level.)

More Difficult General Texts
Basham, A.L., **The Wonder that was India**. London: Fontana 1971
Bonevac, D. & Phillips, S., **Understanding Non-Western Philosophy: Introductory Readings**. California: Mayfield Publishing 1993
Brannigan, M.C., **The Pulse of Wisdom**. Wadsworth Publishing 1995 (Quite dense overview with readings.)
Koller, J.M., **Oriental Philosophies**. New York: Charles Scribner & Sons 1985
Radhakrishnan, S., **Eastern Religions and Western Thought**. Oxford University Press 1992
Riepe, D. (ed), **Asian Philosophy Today**. New York: Gordon & Breach 1981

Hinduism

Brown, B., **The Wisdom of the Hindus**. New York: Garden City Publishing 1938

Hume, R.E., **The Thirteen Principal Upanishads** (2nd edn). Oxford University Press 1983

Isherwood, C. (ed), **Vedanta for the Western World**. London: Unwin Books 1963

Koller, J.M., **The Indian Way**. New York: Macmillan 1982

Moore, C., **The Indian Mind: Essentials of Indian Philosophy and Culture**. University of Hawaii Press 1967

Radhakrishnan, S., **Indian Philosophy** (2 vols). London: Allen & Unwin 1923

Raju, P.T., **The Philosophical Traditions of India**. London: Allen & Unwin 1971

Renou, L., **Religions of Ancient India** New York: Sohocken 1968

Smart, N., **Doctrine and Argument in Indian Philosophy**. London: Allen & Unwin 1964

Zaehner, R.C., **Hindu Scriptures**. London: Everyman's Library, J.M. Dent & Sons 1966

Weber, M., **The Religions of India**. Glencoe, Illinois: 1958

Chinese Philosophy

Allinson, R.E., **Understanding the Chinese Mind**. Hong Kong: Oxford University Press 1989

Bloom, I., **Knowledge Painfully Acquired: The K'un-chih chi by Lo Ch'in-shun**. New York: Columbia University Press 1987

Bodde, D., **Chinese Thought, Society and Science**. University of Hawaii Press 1991

Fung Yu-Lan, **A Short History of Chinese Philosophy**. New York: Free Press 1966 (The most concise and authoritative overview around.)

A History of Chinese Philosophy (2 vols). New Jersey: Princeton University Press 1952

Fung Yu-Lan, **The Spirit of Chinese Philosophy**. London: Routledge, Kegan & Paul 1962

Ch'eng, Chung Ying, **New Dimensions of Confucian and Neo-Confucian Philosophy**. Albany: State University of New York Press 1991

Confucius, **The Analects, The Great Learning and the Doctrine of the Mean**. New York: Dover Publications Inc. 1971

Creel, H.G., **Confucianism and the Chinese Way**. New York: 1960

Chang, Chung-yuan, **Creativity and Taoism**. New York: Harper & Row 1963

Cleary, T., **The Essential Tao**. San Francisco: Harper 1991

The I Ching or Book of Changes. New Jersey: Princeton University Press 1967

Sun Tzu, **The Art of War**. Oxford University Press 1963

Waley, A., **Three Ways of Thought in Ancient China**. London: Allen & Unwin 1939

Richard Osborne

AUTHOR

Ancient Eastern Philosophy

TITLE

for Beginners

DATE